PRAISE FOR *THE ELEVATED*

"*The Elevated Leader* is a powerful guide for anyone ready to rise above old patterns and lead with clarity, purpose, and courage. Laurie Maddalena masterfully blends her real-world leadership experience with transformative insights that inspire growth from the inside out. I've seen firsthand Laurie's passion for helping leaders evolve—and this book reflects the depth of her commitment and wisdom. This book is an invaluable resource for leaders who want to elevate not just their results, but their impact."

—Jack Canfield
Coauthor of the #1 *New York Times* bestselling
Chicken Soup for the Soul® series and
The Success Principles™: *How to Get from*
Where You Are to Where You Want to Be

"*The Elevated Leader* is a standout leadership guide for our time— clear, actionable, and deeply relevant. Laurie Maddalena isn't just teaching leadership; she's challenging outdated habits and offering a fresh, human-centered approach to leading in today's workplace. Her insights are grounded, relatable, and highly valuable for leaders who want to build trust, develop others, and achieve stronger results. I highly recommend this book for any manager looking to lead with more clarity, confidence, and intention."

—Janet Switzer
New York Times bestselling coauthor of
The Success Principles™: *How to Get From*
Where You Are to Where You Want to Be

THE ELEVATED LEADER

BOOST YOUR CONFIDENCE AND TRANSFORM YOUR TEAM BY MASTERING COACHING, ACCOUNTABILITY, AND DIFFICULT CONVERSATIONS

THE ELEVATED LEADER

BOOST YOUR CONFIDENCE AND TRANSFORM YOUR TEAM BY MASTERING COACHING, ACCOUNTABILITY, AND DIFFICULT CONVERSATIONS

BY LAURIE MADDALENA

ethos
collective

Printed in the United States of America

Published by Igniting Souls
PO Box 43, Powell, OH 43065
IgnitingSouls.com

LCCN: 2023921339
Paperback ISBN: 978-1-63680-235-0
Hardcover ISBN: 978-1-63680-236-7
e-book ISBN: 978-1-63680-237-4

Available in paperback, hardcover, e-book, and audiobook.

This book is dedicated to the leaders who choose growth over comfort, intention over habit, and who are building better workplaces—one choice, one action, and one conversation at a time.

TABLE OF CONTENTS

PART 3: LEAD WITH CONFIDENCE, CLARITY, AND RESULTS

FOREWORD
BY KARY OBERBRUNNER

The world is in a constant state of flux. Now, more than ever before, the challenges we face are evolving faster than we can track them. Even just the technological advances we've seen in the past few years have had lasting impacts on the way businesses operate. In such a dynamic environment, leaders who can adapt and evolve with the times succeed, and those who can't get left behind. The world needs more elevated leaders who can take their operating framework to a higher level and possess the skills to inspire, motivate, and empower people to achieve their full potential.

Laurie Maddalena provides the roadmap necessary for leaders to overcome obstacles and experience success. This book is a transformative journey that empowers readers to become influential catalysts within their organizations. It offers real-world examples, actionable insights, and practical advice to create a thriving, positive, results-driven team. And what I most appreciate about Laurie's insights is that she has successfully applied them in her own life.

Laurie highlights the most important skills for leaders to master today, including coaching, accountability, and mastering difficult conversations, among other crucial principles for success. Effective coaching is essential for leaders to help position their employees into high performers who know their purpose and love what they do. The book teaches you how to confidently coach your employees through constant change, harnessing their untapped potential, and guiding them toward greatness.

Instilling accountability is crucial for leaders to hold themselves and their team members accountable for their actions. The book provides insights into how to create a culture of accountability and how to hold yourself and others accountable.

Mastering difficult conversations helps leaders facilitate challenging interactions with grace and effectiveness. The book equips you with the skills to handle even the most difficult exchanges directly and respectfully.

Laurie's framework for cultivating elevated leaders includes the most important skills that I have so often seen lacking in the world today.

If you read this book and take it to heart, you will be giving yourself a platform of stability in your leadership capability that can see you through all the uncertain times ahead. And that stability is not only for you, it's for your business, your employees, your clients, and everyone that your life as a leader touches.

Don't wait. Dive in and apply these principles, because the world needs elevated leaders. The world needs you.

—Kary Oberbrunner
CEO and *Wall Street Journal* and *USA Today*
Bestselling Author

INTRODUCTION

Your mind will take the shape of what you frequently hold in thought, for the human spirit is colored by such impressions.

—Marcus Aurelius, Meditations

One of my summer jobs as a teenager was bussing tables at Danny's Restaurant in my small hometown in upstate New York. One of the owners, Vinny, would occasionally step out of the kitchen to pour himself a Coke at the bar. If he spotted a server, bartender, or busser standing around, he'd say, "If you can lean, you can clean." It was a simple phrase, but it stuck with me.

At the time, I didn't realize how much those seven words would shape my mindset. I quickly learned that staying busy, being helpful, and going above and beyond were not only noticed—they were valued and rewarded. That early lesson taught me to always look for ways to contribute, even when no one was watching.

I took pride in being dependable and hardworking. I showed up early, stayed late, and did more than what was asked. Whether it was opening the ice cream stand on my own (my other job as a teen), taking on extra responsibilities, or earning a promotion, I was consistently recognized for my dedication. In those early years, it felt clear: show up, work hard, stay positive, and your efforts would be recognized and rewarded.

A week after graduating from college, I started work as a customer service representative at an insurance company. It was my first office job; I was excited to wear professional clothes, have my own cubicle, and be given a key card to get into the building. My job was to work the help desk for the IT department, where I answered phones, logged the reason for the call (forgotten password, computer issue, software question), and assigned the problem to one of the four technicians. I worked hard, asked questions, and learned so much about the different software programs we used that, eventually, I could take care of some of the issues myself.

The company had over 500 employees in different locations across the country and was growing fast. A year into the role, the vice president recognized the need for additional support and hired another customer service representative, assigning me as their direct supervisor.

After several interviews, we hired a woman named Pat. Pat was a bubbly woman who was probably about 20 years older than I was. On her first day, she showed up to work with a pad and pen, eager to learn. Pat shadowed me for about a week and then started taking calls herself. From that day on, I figured my job was to give her direction and answer her questions. I wasn't the worst supervisor in the world, but I certainly wasn't the best. I had no idea how to gain respect, develop trust, or keep her engaged. There was no training on how to supervise, and no one explained what was expected of me in this new role. At the time, coaching, employee engagement, managing across generations, and influencing others weren't widely taught or discussed. These weren't standard leadership practices— they simply weren't part of the mainstream conversation in most workplaces, including mine. I had never heard of a class on how to coach or engage people.

I was fortunate to have two strong examples of leadership early on: the vice president and the IT manager. They were kind, approachable, and genuinely enjoyable to be around. They'd often take the team out for lunch at the local pizza or sub shop, asking about our weekends and showing a real interest in our lives. They made a point to recognize good work and express appreciation. I doubt either of them had formal leadership training, but they were both good people who treated others with respect and warmth. The result was a positive, connected departmental culture. Their example showed me that leadership starts with how you treat people.

I supervised Pat for a year before moving from my native New York to Maryland to start fresh. After waiting tables for a year, I secured a job as an assistant manager at the call center of a credit union. I was now supervising 12 member service representatives, and it was very different than supervising Pat. Pat was one person. She was bubbly, receptive, and easy to be around. Frankly, I was lucky to have an easy-going employee as my first direct report. At the credit union, I managed a dozen people with different personalities, experience levels, and ages. I quickly realized that a positive attitude and a great work ethic were not enough to be an effective leader. I felt unprepared and in over my head.

I spent the next several years juggling the demands of managing my team during the day while enrolling in classes and certifications in management, human resources, and leadership outside of work. Through these courses, I gradually built the skills and confidence I needed to manage more effectively. Eventually, I transitioned into the human resources department, where I continued to strengthen my leadership abilities and began creating training programs to help other managers become more effective in their roles.

It's been over 25 years since my first supervisor position at the insurance company, and along the way, I have taken dozens of management and leadership classes and have had the opportunity to teach thousands of professionals the skills and strategies to lead exceptionally. Over time, I noticed a common theme in organizations: People are most often promoted based on their technical skills, rather than their leadership qualities and competencies. The result has been a world of ineffective, unprepared leaders, much like I was when I was first promoted.

It's interesting how training or certifications are expected and typically required in almost every other profession. Pilots, doctors, teachers, artists, cashiers, electricians, and restaurant servers all require training. I received more training to become a server at Dave & Buster's than I ever did at any company I worked for as a leader.

The local barista at Starbucks receives more training and preparation than most leaders in organizations.

Add to that the reality that leadership is always evolving. As workplaces grow more complex and employee expectations continue to rise, managers are expected to operate at a much higher level than ever before, with advanced skills in communication, emotional intelligence, and strategic thinking.

Thirty years ago, many managers could succeed without formal leadership training. Technical expertise, task focus, and clear direction were often enough. Relational and strategic skills weren't seen as essential.

But that approach no longer works. Today's workplace has evolved—there are more women in leadership, greater workforce diversity, and employees have more options than ever before. Modern leadership demands more. It requires emotional intelligence, adaptability, coaching skills, and the ability to inspire and engage people—not just manage tasks.

The traditional, top-down style of leadership is no longer effective. To lead successfully today, managers must be able to connect with people, coach performance, and navigate both challenges and conversations with confidence and care.

 Managers can no longer lead by default; they must lead with intention.

That's why the role of today's leader is more critical than ever—because leadership doesn't just impact performance, it directly shapes the employee experience and well-being.[1] A recent study shows that an employee's manager has just as much impact on their quality of life as their spouse.[2]

Leaders have one of the most important roles in our society. Every day, millions of people go to work feeling disengaged and unhappy. According to Gallup, only 31 percent of employees in the United States are fully engaged at work.[3] As of this writing, that statistic is at a decade low. There is much work to be done. If we upgrade the skills of our managers, we can elevate our culture and the lives of the people we lead.

My vision is to help organizations create cultures where people love to come to work, and workplaces where employees feel valued and appreciated, so they want to bring their best to work each day. This isn't just about having a workplace of happy employees. Having an engaged workforce means higher productivity, less turnover, better service to your customers or members, and higher profits.

It all starts with you. The manager. This book will provide you with the tools for elevating your own personal leadership, whether you are a supervisor, manager, or executive. These strategies will not only make you a better, more impactful leader but will also increase your confidence, reduce stress and burnout, and make your job easier. Yes, easier. Although being a leader is a challenging job, with the right skills, principles, and practices, you can make a bigger impact and leverage your time, energy, and influence more effectively.

The core focus of this book is to cultivate intentional leadership so you can leverage your influence, energy, and focus to facilitate meaningful impact, elevate your team, and create a culture of excellence. My hope is that you will feel inspired to take action on the principles and strategies in this book and see amazing results that will not only elevate your leadership but also elevate your life.

PART 1

THE CASE FOR REVOLUTIONIZING LEADERSHIP

1

THE EVOLUTION OF LEADERSHIP

Change is the law of life. And those who look only to the past or present are certain to miss the future.

—John F. Kennedy

As I was driving my nine-year-old daughter, Olivia, home from an activity one day, she asked curiously what it was like to grow up in the 70s and 80s.

"I'm not sure you would have liked it," I said. "We didn't have phones we could carry around every day—our phone was attached to the wall with a cord, and you had to be home to talk to someone. We also only had a handful of TV channels, not the endless shows and movies you can stream on demand now. And if we wanted to change the channel, we actually had to get up off the couch."

"You mean, when you stood up, the channel changed?" Olivia asked, puzzled.

I laughed. She genuinely thought that just standing up made the channel change. Because in her world, everything is instant, automated, and on demand.

My kids have never had to sit through a commercial or suffer through reruns of Saturday morning cartoons. They have thousands of choices at their fingertips to keep them entertained for their lifetime.

The transformation of technology over the last thirty years has reshaped nearly every aspect of how we live and work. Most of us haven't used a card catalogue in decades; we can order a book from

Amazon.com and have it at our front door tomorrow. We have navigation systems instead of physical maps and smartphones instead of boom boxes (some of you may not even know what I'm talking about!).

I was born in the mid-1970s, and it is astonishing to me how life was for women just one generation before mine. It wasn't until the mid-1970s that women could apply for a credit card or loan in their own name. Prior to that time, a woman had to have her husband's signature to apply for a loan. Women were largely expected to be homemakers or take on supportive roles, with limited financial independence.

Consider these facts about women in the 1970s.[4]

- Women could get fired for becoming pregnant (until 1978).
- Women weren't acknowledged as runners in the Boston Marathon (until 1972).
- Women couldn't be admitted to a military academy (West Point first admitted women in 1976), and they couldn't fight in combat until 2013!
- In many states, a woman couldn't serve as a judge.
- Women couldn't be astronauts (until 1979).
- Ivy League universities didn't regularly accept women until the 1970s. (Yale became the first to admit a woman in 1969. Columbia didn't admit a woman until 1983!)
- Women faced significant barriers not only to gaining admission to law school but also to securing employment afterward, as many law firms were unwilling to hire female graduates.
- Many states didn't allow a woman to serve on a jury until 1973.
- Women didn't have protections to divorce over domestic violence.
- Women weren't CEOs of Fortune 500 companies until Katherine Graham became CEO of *The Washington Post* in 1972.

While we've made meaningful progress over the past 50 years, it's still striking to reflect on how limited women's rights were not so long ago. Although pay equity and access to leadership opportunities remained elusive, the 1970s marked the beginning of a shift. Between 1969 and 1999, the number of women in the workforce more than doubled. Still, traditional management styles dominated, with most leadership roles held by men. And while more women were entering the workplace, they faced persistent barriers—cultural, structural, and systemic.

In the decades that followed, the introduction of the Internet transformed nearly every aspect of work and life. It opened up a world of choices—access to more information, more job opportunities, and a broader view of what a career could look like. With that access came increased competition and rising employee expectations. People were no longer willing to stay in roles where they felt undervalued, unsupported, or stagnant. The employer-employee relationship began to shift in profound ways.

Fast forward to today…

Our world is evolving faster than ever. Technology continues to accelerate, information is instantly accessible, and the leadership skills required today are dramatically different from those valued just a few decades ago.

Thirty years ago, there was little emphasis on engaging employees, coaching direct reports, or intentionally shaping workplace culture. Loyalty and tenure were prized. Many people spent their entire careers at a single organization. Leaders were often transactional—focused on giving directions, solving problems, and delivering results. For a time, that approach worked. But over time, it became clear that simply managing tasks and giving direction wasn't enough—we needed leaders who could connect, coach, and inspire.

Today, leadership is more complex and demanding than ever before. For the first time in history, five generations share the workplace—each with its own set of values, expectations, and communication styles. Navigating this landscape requires far more than technical expertise; it calls for adaptability, empathy, and a deep understanding of how to engage, support, and bring out the best in people.

THE EVOLUTION OF SOCIETY

Technology isn't the only thing that has transformed over the past few decades; our society and families have evolved as well. And with that evolution, expectations around work have shifted significantly.

In my parents' generation, work was primarily a means to support the family. Loyalty and sacrifice were the cornerstones of a strong work ethic. Financial stability often took precedence over personal fulfillment or time spent at home. I grew up in the 1980s watching my dad leave for work at 6 a.m. and return at 6 p.m. every day. Like many men of his generation, he was the primary income earner, while my mom stayed home to raise the kids and manage the household. Their roles were traditional, and their responsibilities were clearly divided.

Even youth sports looked very different back then. Aside from Little League, most kids didn't start organized sports until middle school. Practices and games were typically held right after school, and transportation was often provided, even for away games. Weekends were generally unscheduled and free. I played softball in high school, and my parents never attended a game—not because they weren't supportive, but because it wasn't the norm. Most parents, especially fathers, were focused on earning a living, and attending games during work hours was rare.

Fast forward to today, and the picture has completely changed. Parents are more involved than ever and place a high value on being present in their children's lives. When my son expressed interest in playing baseball at eight years old, another parent told us it might be too late to start. Too late? Many of his teammates had already been in organized leagues since they were five.

With so many opportunities now available, kids are starting younger, and family calendars are packed. Between weeknight practices and weekend games, our family—like many others—spends a significant amount of time juggling sports schedules, school events, and birthday parties. My husband and I, like many working parents today, are constantly navigating how to stay involved while balancing the demands of our own careers.

Societal norms have shifted, parental involvement has increased, traditional roles have become more fluid, and in many households, both parents are now working full-time. At the same time, workplace norms have evolved too. Employees no longer see work as just a paycheck; they want flexibility, fulfillment, and a culture that supports their lives beyond the office. Work is no longer the center of people's identities—it's one part of a more integrated life.

So, what does all of this have to do with leadership?

A lot.

Each generation enters the workforce with a unique set of values and expectations shaped by their upbringing and how they experienced the world around them. While my grandparents' generation prioritized stability and survival, and my parents' generation valued loyalty and financial security, today's workforce places greater emphasis on quality of life, flexibility, and career growth opportunities. With both parents often working and more women in the workplace than ever before, traditional roles have shifted, and so have priorities.

Understanding these generational shifts is essential for modern leaders. Because today, people aren't just looking for a paycheck—they're looking for purpose, growth, and balance. And leaders who recognize and respond to these evolving expectations are the ones who will truly engage and retain top talent.

Yet not everything has evolved as quickly as employee expectations. We still have generations in the workforce that were conditioned to value loyalty, sacrifice, and tenure. Success often meant long hours at the office and visible busyness. As more women entered the workforce, they too felt the pressure to keep up and prove themselves through sheer effort and time. Over the years, this mindset created workplace cultures that rewarded hustle and overwork. Busyness became a badge of honor, and productivity was often measured in hours rather than impact. And while the world around us has changed, remnants of this outdated operating system still linger today.

Then came a shift.

As Millennials entered the workforce, they brought a different set of values, questioning the old model. Many viewed their push for flexibility, purpose, and balance as entitlement. They were often labeled bold, lazy, or disloyal. But in truth, much of what they challenged needed to be challenged. Millennials helped move the workplace forward by demanding a more human, values-aligned approach to work. Still, their vision often clashed with the beliefs and expectations of previous generations, creating inevitable tension.

In a recent leadership workshop I facilitated, we explored these generational dynamics and the changing expectations of today's workforce. One manager admitted, "This is really hard. Managing people who want more connection, coaching, and development takes a lot of time." And they're right—it is hard. Being a leader today demands more energy, attention, and intentional effort than ever before.

Leadership today is more complex than ever. In addition to rising expectations for personal growth and emotional intelligence, leaders are navigating remote and hybrid work, shifting business models, and a faster pace of change. It's no longer enough to direct and delegate. Today's leaders must invest more time, energy, and intentionality into caretaking the culture of their team.

It was far simpler in the days of transactional management, when employees showed up, did their jobs, and went home. But those days are gone. Today's workplace demands a new kind of leadership; one built on connection, adaptability, and a genuine commitment to people.

When I first entered the workforce thirty years ago, leadership development looked very different. You didn't hear much about workshops on coaching, employee engagement, or emotional intelligence. The workplace was more traditional: if you didn't hear from your manager, it usually meant you were doing fine. Ongoing feedback was rare unless something was wrong, and career development plans were typically reserved for executives. Most people came to work, put in their 40 or 50 hours, and collected a paycheck. That was the norm, and few questioned it.

The reality is, we can't slow down or reverse this evolution. Longing for the way things used to be or resisting the realities of a modern workplace is not an effective leadership strategy. And yet, many managers find themselves stuck, overwhelmed, or frustrated because they are trying to lead with an outdated model in a rapidly changing world.

To thrive in this new environment, leaders must be agile and forward-thinking. They must guide themselves and their teams through constant change with clarity, empathy, and purpose. Unfortunately, many individuals and organizations still rely on leadership practices that don't engage, inspire, or deliver meaningful results.

THE PERSISTENCE OF MEDIOCRE LEADERSHIP

Over the past thirty years, nearly everything has transformed. We can order groceries with a tap on our phones, stream brand-new movies from our living rooms, and access answers to almost any question in seconds.

And yet, one thing has remained remarkably unchanged: mediocre leadership.

Despite rapid advances in technology and shifts in how we live and work, outdated leadership styles still dominate. Yes, there are bold, forward-thinking leaders—but they remain the exception. Across industries, uninspiring, transactional leadership remains deeply embedded in organizational culture.

Why does mediocrity persist? Because most workplace cultures are built to maintain it. Think of culture like a thermostat: when someone turns up the heat with bold thinking, innovation, or a challenge to the status quo, the system automatically works to return to its comfortable setting. Unless the culture itself is intentionally rewired, mediocrity becomes the default—and even high performers are pulled back into the norm.

While many organizations have been slow to evolve, today's employees have not. Workers now expect more from their jobs: more meaning, more development, more flexibility, and more purpose. Traditional leadership approaches based on authority, control, or blind loyalty fall flat in today's environment. Managers can no longer just give orders and solve problems. They must coach, inspire, and foster collaboration to drive both growth and results.

At the same time, leaders are managing more complexity than ever. Dual-career households are now the norm, and generational shifts have redefined what people want from work. Leadership today requires the ability to build trust, adapt quickly, and connect meaningfully.

A high-performance culture begins at the top.

It takes bold, courageous CEOs, executives, and managers to reset the cultural thermostat and declare that mediocrity is no longer acceptable. Exceptional leaders don't just talk about culture; they demonstrate it through their everyday leadership decisions, actions, and presence. They lead with clarity and conviction, creating environments where people can thrive, grow, and perform at their best.

SIGNS OF A MEDIOCRE CULTURE

Mediocre Leaders vs. Exceptional Leaders

Mediocre Leaders	Exceptional Leaders
Spend more time and energy disciplining or tolerating low performers than developing top talent. Avoid crucial conversations or handle them with a command-and-control approach. Miss opportunities to coach and elevate performance.	Focus on coaching employees to peak performance. Step in to support and coach when standards aren't met. Make tough decisions when necessary because they understand the cultural impact of tolerating low performance.
Avoid confrontation because they find it uncomfortable. Reward compliance over honesty and candor. Hesitate to take action, make excuses for poor performance, and prefer to avoid rocking the boat.	Have the courage to address difficult situations early. Recognize that uncomfortable conversations are necessary to maintain high standards and long-term team success. Take action rather than delay.

Rely on outdated, command-and-control methods. Micromanage and lead through fear. Believe the paycheck is the reward and undervalue feedback, empathy, appreciation, and engagement. Miss the connection between employee experience and results.	Lead with a modern, people-centered approach. Prioritize coaching, feedback, appreciation, and support. Foster an environment of collaboration and trust by adjusting their style to meet employees' needs.
Prefer technical work over leadership responsibilities. Spend most of their time putting out fires, handling interruptions, or doing individual contributor work. Complain about a lack of time for coaching and planning, but resist shifting into a strategic mindset.	Understand that their value lies in how they lead, not what they produce technically. Prioritize developing others, setting direction, and staying focused on long-term goals. Delegate well and create clarity through consistent communication.
Struggle to retain high performers. Accept average performance as the norm, which frustrates top employees. Their tolerance of mediocrity causes high performers to disengage or leave the organization.	Set high expectations and challenge their teams to grow. Invest time in keeping top performers engaged and appreciated. Send a clear message that excellence is the standard, and average is not acceptable.

If you tolerate mediocrity and fail to reward excellence, your culture will stay average. But by setting higher standards, recognizing top performers, and coaching or transitioning low performers, you can transform your culture over time.

One of the biggest challenges in organizations today is that many managers are not equipped to lead effectively in a rapidly evolving workplace. While work expectations have changed, many leaders have not kept pace. The outdated practice of promoting based on technical expertise has weakened workplace cultures, leaving transactional management as the norm rather than the exception.

Redefining Leadership for a Changing World

To build a thriving, high-performing organization, leaders must develop the mindset, self-awareness, and skills needed to navigate today's complexities. Fortunately, you can elevate both your leadership and your organization's culture. In this book, we will explore the key strategies and practices needed to thrive in today's evolving workplace.

Leadership isn't easy—it demands a relentless focus on people and the organization. It requires courageous conversations for the sake of the culture. Exceptional leaders act as cultural caretakers, knowing that every decision shapes the workplace. They make the choice every day to lead at a higher level.

Leadership must evolve. It's time to set a higher standard, one where leaders prioritize respect, connection, and well-being while also facilitating accountability and exceptional results.

2

NOT EVERYONE IS MEANT
TO BE A LEADER

We rise by lifting others. If service is below you,
leadership is beyond you.
—Robert G. Ingersoll

One weekend, my kids decided to put on a play in our living room. Olivia, my oldest, quickly assumed the director role by assigning parts, telling everyone where to stand, and dismissing any ideas that didn't match her vision. What started as a fun and imaginative activity unraveled within minutes. Luca and Clara grew frustrated, and before long, tears were flowing. The play ended before it ever began.

Olivia came to me, clearly upset. "They won't listen!" she said, exasperated. I could see how frustrated she was, and it felt like a teachable moment—an opportunity to talk about what real leadership looks like. I told her, "People don't follow dictators. If you want your brother and sister to follow you, they need to feel included. Being the leader isn't about being bossy, it's about involving them and listening to their ideas."

As leadership has evolved, so has the language we use to describe potential. You may have heard the well-meaning advice that we should stop calling girls "bossy" and instead recognize those behaviors as leadership. While I understand the intention—especially in a society where girls have often been conditioned to be agreeable—I don't entirely agree. Bossy is not leadership.

Leadership is not about control, dominance, or giving orders. Effective leadership is about influence, collaboration, and creating space for others to contribute.

If we want to grow strong, effective leaders in our homes, schools, or organizations, we must be clear about what leadership *is* and what it *isn't*. True leadership is built on service, not control. It's about inspiring, empowering, and connecting, not commanding.

We've all experienced individuals in leadership roles who aren't truly leading. A title or promotion doesn't make someone a leader. Leadership isn't granted—it's earned through growth, self-awareness, and consistent action. You become a leader by how you show up, how you influence and inspire others, and how you respond to challenges. It's not just about managing tasks or setting goals—it's about building trust, communicating clearly, making thoughtful decisions, and supporting your team through coaching and development.

> LEADERSHIP IS NOT ABOUT CONTROL, DOMINANCE, OR GIVING ORDERS. EFFECTIVE LEADERSHIP IS ABOUT INFLUENCE, COLLABORATION, AND CREATING SPACE FOR OTHERS TO CONTRIBUTE.

Exceptional leaders are committed to continuous growth—not just to sharpen their skills, but to expand their impact. They look beyond themselves, striving to make a meaningful difference in their teams, their organizations, and the world around them. Leadership is not just about learning new tools or techniques; it's about adopting a new way of thinking, showing up differently, and leading with intention.

At its core, true leadership is about service. It means serving your employees by investing in their growth and helping them reach their full potential. It means serving your organization by contributing your best to its mission and goals. And it means serving your customers or members by keeping their needs at the center and helping them succeed.

Many people focus on what they will gain when they step into a leadership role—more authority, a bigger salary, a prestigious title.

But few pause to consider what they are meant to give. Leadership is both a privilege and a responsibility. It's not about the power you hold, but the impact you have. True leadership is about service, influence, and the responsibility to create an environment where people can thrive and succeed. And not everyone has the skills to facilitate that kind of work environment.

> NOT EVERYONE IS
> MEANT TO BE A LEADER.

Not everyone is meant to be a leader.

Just like not everyone is meant to be a teacher, a pilot, a customer service representative (have you experienced someone who definitely should NOT be in customer service? 😵), an architect, or a barista, not everyone is meant to be a leader. Yet many companies still follow the old practice of promoting the technical superstar to a leadership position.

Yes, you can lead at any level of the organization, and anyone can exhibit leadership qualities, even without a formal title. But context is important. Not everyone is meant to be a leader of people. The skills required to lead effectively today are much higher than ever before. It takes emotional intelligence, exceptional communication skills, the ability to navigate complexity, and a genuine passion for developing others. We need to make it acceptable, and even respected, for professionals to opt out of people leadership if it's not the right fit. Because leadership isn't just a promotion, it's a responsibility.

When I worked at a credit union, our CEO approached me one day and said, "You should promote Eve to HR Manager—she's fantastic." And she was. Eve was one of our top performers in her role as an HR Generalist. She was dependable, thoughtful, knowledgeable, and highly respected across the organization. On paper, she looked like the perfect candidate for leadership.

But when I brought the idea to Eve, she didn't hesitate. "I appreciate the confidence," she said, "but I'm not interested in a management role." She went on to explain that while she loved her work and cared deeply about the organization, she knew she wouldn't enjoy managing people, and didn't feel like those were her strongest skills—or ones she wanted to develop. Leadership didn't align with her personality, talents, or passion. She genuinely loved her role and wanted to continue growing and developing within it, just not by moving into management. She wasn't drawn to having difficult conversations, navigating team dynamics, or giving feedback—skills that are essential in leadership. She had a deep understanding of her strengths, her preferences, and where she did her best work.

I really admired her level of self-awareness and maturity. Eve didn't equate career growth with climbing the management ladder. She wasn't chasing a title; she was committed to excellence in a position that was a great match for her skills, goals, and passion. And because she had clarity about what she wanted (and didn't want), she thrived. She brought full engagement and high performance to her role, not because she was trying to move up, but because she found meaning and mastery in what she did.

Too often, employees pursue leadership roles by default, assuming that advancement must lead to managing others. But leadership is not the right path for everyone—and that's okay. Eve is a reminder that success doesn't always mean stepping into a higher title. Sometimes, the most powerful choice is knowing where you can contribute most and having the confidence to pursue a career path that truly aligns with your skills and passion. While many leadership skills can be taught, true success in a leadership role also requires a genuine desire to lead, the right temperament, and a passion for developing and supporting others.

We need technically proficient, high-performing individual contributors just as much as we need great people leaders. Both roles are essential to a thriving organization. The key is making sure we're not promoting people simply because they excel in their current role, especially if the next step doesn't align with their strengths or aspirations. When we place someone in a leadership role they're not suited for, we risk diminishing their performance, undermining their confidence, and weakening the culture around them.

Success isn't about following a single path; it's about finding the right fit. And as leaders, it's our responsibility to support that clarity in others and to create growth opportunities that honor both individual strengths and organizational needs. We need to create meaningful career paths that don't require stepping into leadership so high-performing individuals can continue to grow, contribute, and be recognized without having to manage people.

To elevate our cultures, we should stop promoting employees for technical expertise and start promoting them for leadership qualities. This means we need to invest time and energy into coaching our employees and preparing them for leadership positions BEFORE they move into the role. Not everyone possesses the competencies necessary to lead a team effectively.

> SUCCESS ISN'T ABOUT FOLLOWING A SINGLE PATH; IT'S ABOUT FINDING THE RIGHT FIT.

Most managers don't receive any formal training before being promoted into a leadership role. That was certainly the case for me. As I mentioned previously, I received no training for my first official leadership position as a supervisor at the IT help desk. It took time, experience, and eventually formal training for me to fully understand that being an exceptional leader wasn't about giving instructions and answering questions.

I've seen many people have this experience: They are promoted to a leadership role without fully understanding what it takes to be successful. Whether you are currently in a leadership role or aspire to a leadership position one day, I want to offer some guidance on how to tell if leadership is or is not the best career path for you or your employees.

How can you tell if leadership is *or is not* the best career path for you or your employees?

Five Signs That You Should Not Be a Leader

1. **You prefer to work alone.**

   Cultivating relationships is the foundation of inspiring people to make their best contribution, which is not conducive to working alone.

   Leadership is about facilitating others to bring out their best and help them achieve individual and organizational goals. This requires consistent coaching, supporting, and recognition of employees.

   Exceptional leaders don't see these as duties they somehow have to fit into their busy schedule and workload; they see them as a responsibility to foster the potential in each employee and the team. Exceptional leaders realize that spending time with their people is a great investment toward mutual success. It's okay to prefer to work alone, but that probably means you shouldn't be a leader.

2. **You avoid confrontation.**

   There are some universal truths in leadership: People will not always meet expectations, and things will not always go as planned.

   While most people don't like confrontation, great leaders must have the courage to facilitate challenging conversations for the sake of the team. As a manager, you will often need to approach uncomfortable situations with your employees, your colleagues, and even your boss.

   Exceptional leaders don't avoid these situations; they see them as a necessary step for working through issues and moving forward. Leaders may never enjoy these conversations, but they learn the skills necessary to facilitate them effectively.

3. **You prefer doing technical work.**

Leadership is about getting results through people, not by yourself.

One of the biggest challenges that holds leaders back from being successful is the inability to delegate. Many leaders who were superstars in a contributor role struggle to resist using their technical expertise and getting into the weeds. But the competencies needed to be successful in a leadership role are very different from those in a technical role. If you prefer doing technical work, that's a good sign that you should remain in a technical role where you can shine.

4. **You consider the human side of business less important than metrics and results.**

Leading means investing in people, having the hard conversations, and doing the work necessary to create an environment where both individuals and the organization thrive.

More than ever, leadership is about more than just overseeing tasks; it's about coaching, developing talent, fostering collaboration, holding regular meetings to build alignment, and ensuring that every team member is engaged and performing at their best. Successful leadership balances two critical elements: facilitating results and creating a positive, engaged team. You cannot build a high-performing team without both.

Engagement leads to higher productivity, which leads to better results. Exceptional leaders spend most of their time developing and supporting their employees. What have traditionally been called "soft skills" are, in reality, essential skills—critical to a leader's ability to inspire, engage, and facilitate meaningful results. If you believe that employee engagement isn't worth your time and effort, or you wouldn't enjoy focusing on these elements on a daily basis, then leadership isn't the right path for you.

5. **You'd rather fix than coach.**

Great leaders facilitate exceptional performance from their teams by instilling ownership and accountability in others through coaching, support, and guidance, helping them reach their potential and create results. This takes time, energy, and effort, and it requires *leaders to frequently adjust their style* to be effective with employees' different preferences and personalities.

If you'd prefer to fix problems and accomplish daily activities rather than spend time guiding, supporting, and coaching others to elicit their highest potential (and to fix the problems themselves), that's a good sign that you should *not* be a leader.

In my work with executives and managers, I have found several characteristics that influential leaders possess.

- **A dedication to continuous learning**: Influential leaders strive to improve every day. They read books and articles, listen to inspiring resources, and seek to gain more information about their industry, as well as how to become a better leader and improve as a person. They are very self-aware; they understand their strengths and weaknesses and are not afraid to hire others to fill the gaps. Always in a state of learning, they also encourage their employees to grow and develop.

- **A focus on others:** Influential leaders aren't in leadership for themselves; they are there to make an impact on others. They provide clarity, direction, appreciation, and support to their employees. Employees are their priority, and they invest time and effort into helping each individual reach their peak performance and potential. They are not afraid to provide constructive feedback, for they know it's about facilitating improvement and is in service to the greater good.

- **Emotional intelligence:** Influential leaders recognize that great leadership extends beyond driving the agenda and achieving results. They understand the importance of people, and they are approachable, compassionate, supportive, and great listeners. They understand that employees are people who have desires, goals, and fears.

- **High integrity**: Even in the midst of organizational change and uncertainty, influential leaders cultivate an environment of stability. Dependability, honesty, trustworthiness, and respectfulness are key characteristics of these leaders. They follow through on their word and possess a high level of integrity. While they don't have all the answers, they are not afraid to admit it and are forthcoming about the mistakes they make. Integrity and trust are reinforced through the behaviors they model.

Certainly, effective leaders need talent, confidence, and strategic ability. But what truly separates exceptional leaders from mediocre ones are the qualities that go beyond technical expertise and strategic mastery. The best leaders cultivate an environment of trust, engagement, loyalty, and growth, fostering a culture where both people and performance thrive.

We need a higher standard for leadership, one that ensures the right individuals step into leadership roles for the right reasons. A key step in elevating your team and organizational culture is breaking the outdated cycle of promoting technical superstars into leadership without assessing their ability to lead or providing them with the necessary training and support. CEOs, executives, and managers can take two critical actions to change this.

First, stop promoting people solely based on technical expertise and instead prioritize those with the mindset, skills, and commitment to lead. Second, provide a transparent preview of leadership before making promotions. Provide employees with opportunities to understand key leadership responsibilities, such as coaching, managing diverse personalities, fostering team dynamics, and navigating tough conversations, so they can make an informed decision about whether leadership is the right path for them. Raising the bar for leadership strengthens organizations, engages teams, and builds a thriving workplace culture.

Leadership isn't for everyone, and that's okay. We must normalize opting out of leadership and stop assuming it's the default next step for every high performer. Leadership roles should be filled by those who are genuinely invested in developing others and facilitating team success, not just those with technical expertise. There are many ways to make a meaningful impact without leading people, and organizations must recognize and value those contributions just as highly.

Recognizing what it takes to be an effective leader is just the beginning. Even with the right mindset and intentions, certain pitfalls can undermine leadership effectiveness. In the next chapter, we'll explore the six biggest leadership saboteurs—barriers that can hold leaders back from success and prevent them from reaching leadership excellence.

3

THE SIX LEADERSHIP SABOTEURS

Knowing yourself is the beginning of all wisdom.

—Aristotle

I began my career in human resources as an HR generalist at a credit union, a position focused on the technical aspects of HR with no management responsibilities. I processed payroll every two weeks, enrolled new hires in our benefit program, ensured compliance with federal and state employment laws, and assisted managers in navigating employee challenges. I loved this job. I found great satisfaction in learning and mastering new tasks and expanding my HR skills. During that first year, my confidence grew, and I worked hard to become indispensable to my manager, Deb, the vice president of Human Resources.

Because of my hard work, Deb promoted me to assistant director of Human Resources. I was thrilled. I now had two employees reporting directly to me, and I was excited to continue to build my leadership skills. Deb was a truly supportive and motivating manager, consistently making me feel recognized and confident in the quality of my work. I was eager to embrace this new challenge and contribute even more to the team's success.

Three months into my new position, Deb gave me some feedback that, looking back now, was instrumental in my leadership development. It was a casual conversation, but I took it to heart and felt like I wasn't performing up to expectations. Deb told me that she noticed I was still mostly doing my old responsibilities from my HR generalist role, and that she wanted me to start focusing on more strategic projects, like creating training programs for our managers. Essentially, I was getting into the weeds and still doing much of the technical work from my previous job, which was holding me back from being effective in my new leadership role.

Frankly, it hadn't occurred to me that doing parts of my old job was getting in the way of my success in my new position. I was focused on being of value to each employee, which was essential for success in my previous job. If an employee called about a mistake on their paycheck, instead of delegating it to one of my team members, I fixed it myself. If an employee had a question about their benefits, I thought it would be rude to tell them to call one of my team members, so I handled it myself. What I didn't notice was that these seemingly small requests were taking up so much of my time that I was essentially still doing my old job. While I was serving the employee who called me, I was not being of service to the organization.

I thought my technical skills were the value I brought to the organization, and that was true for my old position. But in my new role, it was my leadership skills that contributed the most value to the organization. Deb wanted me to shift my focus from the technical aspects of HR to the more strategic areas where I could make a bigger impact, such as developing training workshops.

I'm so grateful that Deb gave me this constructive feedback early in this new role, so I could shift my focus and energy into the elements of the position that would make me successful.

TRANSITIONING TO LEADERSHIP

In my leadership consulting work, one of the most common challenges I see managers face when transitioning into leadership roles is shifting from the technical expertise that earned them recognition as individual contributors to developing the leadership competencies necessary for success in their new position.

This can be especially hard for leaders who were promoted from within. It's very easy and tempting to keep doing what you were doing before because you know how to do your team members' jobs. In addition, these were the skills you used to earn the promotion, and we naturally think that continuing to use those skills will lead to more success.

CHALLENGES OF TRANSITIONING TO A LEADERSHIP ROLE

1. **Transitioning into a leadership role can feel overwhelming and uncertain.** More often than not, new managers aren't provided training on where to focus their time and energy for successful leadership. Since most managers receive no training or preparation before assuming leadership roles, they often struggle to transition from doing to leading, particularly in higher-level, strategic work. In fact, it's common in my coaching conversations to hear executives ask, "How do I become more strategic? What exactly does that look like?" or, "I'm not sure what my CEO means when she says I need to lead instead of manage."

   And it's not just new managers who struggle. Even tenured leaders can feel overwhelmed by the evolving expectations of leadership today. The bar has been raised, and many experienced leaders have never received training in the more modern, people-centered skills now required for success, like coaching, emotional intelligence, communication, flexibility, and agility.

   We've been conditioned to be doers, focused on completing tasks and checking boxes to feel productive. Leadership, on the other hand, isn't as easily measured by a checklist. While there are specific actions that contribute to effective leadership, the work is often more nuanced, relational, and long-term. It doesn't offer the same immediate sense of accomplishment. That's why many managers naturally gravitate toward task-based work, because checking something off a list gives us a quick hit of satisfaction, even if it doesn't move the needle strategically.

2. **In many organizations, leadership development simply isn't prioritized**—often not because it's unimportant, but because attention is directed toward more immediate, tangible business demands. As a result, managers are rarely taught how to lead effectively, and many executives themselves were never formally trained in modern leadership practices. This creates a cycle that continues until organizations become more intentional about how they promote and prepare future leaders. Elevating someone based solely on technical excellence is common, but without the right development and support, even high-potential employees can struggle in leadership roles.

3. **In traditional work environments, managers were trained and rewarded for solving problems and maintaining output.** This approach worked for a long time; leaders could be considered effective simply by keeping operations running smoothly. But as discussed in the previous chapter, the world of work has changed. Employees today want more than direction; they want growth, connection, purpose, and support.

   The traditional leadership style that once worked is no longer effective. Many tenured leaders who were successful earlier in their careers are now struggling to meet the demands of a modern workforce. In many cases, they haven't evolved their skills to keep pace with what leadership requires today. As a result, senior leaders often lack the ability to coach their managers on how to lead more effectively—perpetuating outdated habits that create a cycle of disengagement.

Even leaders who understand they should be focusing on the leadership aspects of their role often struggle to let go of the day-to-day tasks. The pull to stay in the weeds is strong: completing small tasks and resolving urgent issues can create the illusion of productivity. But these activities rarely create meaningful, long-term results. Instead, they keep leaders reactive and distracted from the work that truly moves the needle.

These managers often tell themselves there's no time to coach, connect, or provide feedback; not because they don't care, but because they've become conditioned to prioritize urgency over impact. They haven't yet developed the mindset or skills needed to shift into the higher-value work of leadership.

Remaining focused on technical tasks limits a leader's ability to make the critical shift required to thrive in a leadership role. As a result, both new and experienced managers often neglect the very competencies that define great leadership: coaching their team, building strong relationships, facilitating results through others, adapting their style, and delegating effectively. The problem isn't always motivation; it's preparation. Most managers were never taught how to lead, so it's only natural that they revert to the habits and tactics that brought them success in previous roles.

I refer to this as "managing by default." It's when leaders stay stuck in the weeds, continuing to perform tasks they've always done, instead of focusing on the bigger picture of leadership. Operating in this way undermines a leader's potential and hinders their success. While there are many habits that can hold leaders back, I've found that there are six key areas—what I call the **Six Leadership Saboteurs**—that consistently prevent managers from becoming the influential, effective leaders they aspire to be. And all of these saboteurs share one common thread: they often arise from an overemphasis on technical expertise and focus.

The reality is, nearly every leader will struggle with one or several of these saboteurs at some point in their career. This isn't a sign of failure; it's a natural part of the leadership journey. The true risk lies in being unaware of these patterns. When left unchecked, they quietly erode your influence, your effectiveness, and the team culture you're trying to build. But when you become aware of them, you gain the power to shift. You can address them directly, develop through them, and lead with greater clarity, intention, and impact. Leadership isn't about perfection; it's about self-awareness, a commitment to growth, and a willingness to be open to feedback.

THE SIX LEADERSHIP SABOTEURS

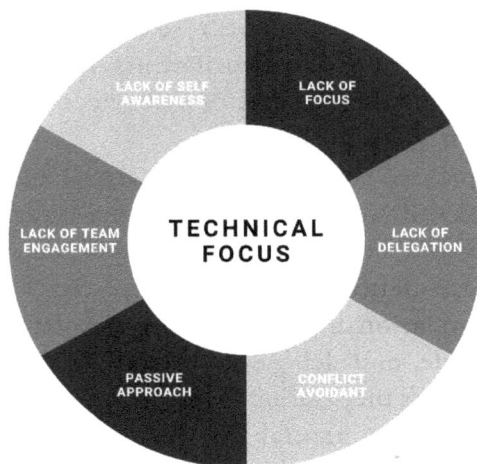

1. Lack of Self-Awareness

   o Unaware of how their behavior impacts others
   o Reacts instead of reflects
   o Relies on outdated leadership habits

2. Lack of Focus

   o Spends too much time in the weeds
   o Prioritizes tasks over people and strategy
   o Struggles to focus on what creates impactful results

3. Lack of Delegation

- ○ Holds onto technical work and control
- ○ Believes their value comes from doing, not leading
- ○ Hesitates to trust others with important tasks

4. Lack of Team Engagement

- ○ Focuses on tasks more than people
- ○ Leads through transactions, not relationships
- ○ Avoids addressing performance and engagement issues

5. Conflict Avoidant

- ○ Avoids difficult conversations to keep the peace
- ○ Ignores underperformance and team tension
- ○ Allows issues to linger instead of addressing them early

6. Passive approach

- ○ Fails to provide clear direction or feedback
- ○ Rarely recognizes or appreciates good work
- ○ Waits to react instead of leading proactively

1. LACK OF SELF-AWARENESS

Most leaders want to be effective, respected, and impactful, but that starts with understanding how they show up. The ability to be self-aware is foundational to exceptional leadership. Leaders with the Lack of Self-Awareness saboteur struggle to see how their behavior, tone, and decisions impact others. If you don't have an accurate view of yourself, you'll miss critical opportunities for growth, connection, and influence.

Self-awareness starts with curiosity and reflection. Without it, you may unintentionally repeat unhelpful patterns, dismiss valuable feedback, or believe you're more effective than you truly are. Many leaders operate this way—on autopilot, unaware of how they're perceived or how their actions affect the culture and results of their team.

Understanding your own strengths, weaknesses, working style, and preferences is crucial to leading effectively. Without this level of self-awareness, it's nearly impossible to build strong relationships, foster trust, or create a high-performing team. Leaders with the Lack of Self-Awareness saboteur are often unaware of how their behavior impacts those around them, and that disconnect can erode team performance and culture.

> SELF-AWARENESS STARTS WITH CURIOSITY AND REFLECTION.

This saboteur can show up in many ways. Some leaders micromanage, controlling every detail because they don't realize how their lack of trust stifles autonomy. Others dominate conversations, talk over people, or fail to listen, often without realizing how this discourages input and shuts down collaboration. Some leaders take their stress out on others, responding with impatience or frustration that damages morale. These behaviors may seem minor in the moment, but over time, they build resentment, disengagement, and mistrust.

In other cases, the effects are more subtle: a leader who rarely makes eye contact, who doesn't ask for feedback, or who unknowingly dismisses ideas can still have a negative impact, even if they don't intend to. Whether overt or passive, a lack of self-awareness limits a leader's ability to connect, adapt, and influence—skills that are essential in today's workplace.

Becoming a more self-aware leader starts with the willingness to pause, reflect, and ask: *How do others experience me? What impact do I want to have—and is my behavior aligned with that?*

Most of us begin our careers as individual contributors, where success is measured by technical skills, task completion, and individual results. While we may collaborate with others, the focus is primarily on our own performance. Without regular feedback—both positive and constructive—we often remain unaware of how our style affects those around us.

When individuals lacking self-awareness are promoted into leadership roles, the impact of their behaviors becomes amplified. What might have been a minor irritation as a peer—interrupting, micromanaging, or being overly critical—can become far more damaging when it comes from a manager.

It's one thing to work alongside someone with poor self-awareness; it's another to report to them. A negative or unaware leader can undermine confidence, engagement, and performance across an entire team.

We'll explore how to build greater self-awareness in a later chapter.

COMMON EXAMPLES THAT CONTRIBUTE TO LACK OF SELF-AWARENESS

- Not asking for feedback or only asking people who won't challenge you
- Dismissing feedback as untrue or irrelevant without reflection
- Failing to reflect on how your behavior affects others
- Talking more than listening in conversations
- Being unaware of your emotional triggers or reactions
- Assuming your intent always matches your impact
- Not noticing how your tone or body language may be perceived
- Believing you're approachable while your team avoids bringing you concerns
- Ignoring signs of disengagement or frustration on your team
- Leading from habit or ego rather than intention and growth

---

2. LACK OF FOCUS

Most leaders struggle to prioritize their many projects and tasks, and frequently feel overwhelmed. The ability to focus is one of the most essential skills for leadership today. I believe it's the foundation for exceptional leadership. Leaders with the Lack of Focus saboteur struggle to manage their energy and focus. If you are not focused on the Key Result Areas of your position, you will never find time for the important aspects of leadership, like coaching, providing feedback, building connections, and developing your team.

Focus begins with clarity. Without a clear understanding of your strategic priorities, departmental goals, or daily objectives, you'll find yourself spinning your wheels, reacting to issues, putting out fires, and staying busy without making meaningful progress. Yet this is how most leaders operate every day.

COMMON EXAMPLES THAT CONTRIBUTE TO LACK OF FOCUS

- Allowing emergencies and interruptions to dictate your day
- Not prioritizing your to-do list and focusing on low-value tasks
- Not being intentional about how you will spend your time (no plan for your day)
- Allowing too many distractions and interruptions
- Having your email open all day
- Not blocking time in your calendar to focus on Key Result Areas
- Not scheduling priorities in your calendar
- Focusing on small tasks that keep you in activity mode rather than accomplishment mode

---

Most leaders are activity-focused rather than results-focused. They stay busy, but not always on what matters most. A lack of clarity at the leadership level leads to confusion across the team, leaving employees uncertain about priorities and spending their time on work that doesn't contribute to the best results.

You can be intelligent, strategic, and emotionally aware, but if you're not able to focus on the right work or guide your team to do the same, you won't be effective. Without intentionality, your day quickly

> MOST LEADERS ARE ACTIVITY-FOCUSED RATHER THAN RESULTS-FOCUSED.

fills with interruptions and low-value tasks, pulling you away from your most critical responsibility as a leader: caretaking the culture.

Caretaking the culture means coaching your team, providing clear direction and feedback, building strong relationships, ensuring alignment around priorities, and developing your people. This is the work that fosters high performance and engagement, but only if you create the space and clarity to prioritize it.

3. LACK OF TEAM ENGAGEMENT

Many leaders assume their team is engaged because no one is complaining, deadlines are being met, and things appear to be running smoothly. But true engagement goes deeper than surface-level performance. Leaders with the Lack of Team Engagement saboteur often miss subtle signals of disconnection, low morale, or untapped potential. They may be focused on tasks and results but neglect the relational aspects that foster trust, commitment, and ownership.

In addition, because most leaders feel overloaded and overwhelmed, they often move through their days in reactive mode rather than with intention. These managers rarely make time for coaching or developing their people, or they avoid it altogether because they're unsure how to do it effectively. But today's employees, especially your high performers, expect more. They want to grow, feel valued, and see a path forward. When leaders neglect to build relationships, give meaningful feedback, and coach employees toward their potential, the result is low engagement, high turnover, and a culture of mediocrity.

Engagement doesn't happen by accident—it's created through intentional leadership. When leaders fail to check in, recognize effort, or create space for meaningful dialogue, team members begin to feel like order takers rather than essential contributors.

COMMON EXAMPLES THAT CONTRIBUTE TO A LACK OF TEAM ENGAGEMENT

- Not getting to know your employees as individuals
- Not prioritizing coaching, feedback, and appreciation
- Not providing meaningful feedback
- Neglecting to coach and develop your employees
- Only checking in with employees when something goes wrong
- Rarely asking for input or ideas from the team
- Failing to recognize or acknowledge individual contributions
- Not creating space for regular team dialogue or connection
- Assuming silence equals agreement or satisfaction
- Over-relying on task management rather than relationship building
- Making decisions in isolation without involving the team
- Not noticing or addressing signs of burnout, frustration, and underperformance

---

In the traditional work environment, these elements of leadership were not valued as they are today. Again, this is why we have many ineffective managers and executives who have not evolved and upgraded their leadership skills to continue to be effective. The result is that many tenured managers have failed to adapt to these crucial elements of leadership, rendering them ineffective. To be an effective leader today, it is essential to prioritize individual and team engagement.

4. LACK OF DELEGATION

Many leaders fall into the trap of doing too much themselves. Whether it's because they can do it faster, don't trust others to do it "right," or feel guilty assigning tasks, the result is the same: burnout and bottlenecks. Leaders with the Lack of Delegation saboteur stay too involved in the day-to-day, often at the expense of strategic thinking, coaching, and developing others. Delegation isn't just about offloading tasks; it's about empowering your team, building trust, and creating space for you to lead at a higher level.

Delegation can feel uncomfortable at first. It requires letting go of control and being okay with things being done differently than you would do them. But without it, you limit your team's growth and your own leadership potential. Over time, a lack of delegation leads to micromanagement, disengaged employees, and a leader who feels overwhelmed and stuck in the weeds.

The ability to delegate is one of the most important habits of successful leadership. In fact, Lack of Delegation is often one of the main reasons leaders aren't successful. Leaders with the Lack of Delegation saboteur get satisfaction and a sense of accomplishment from technical work, so they often don't have time to focus on the important leadership elements.

Leading at a strategic level is necessary for effective leadership. Yet, for many people, the strategic elements of leadership, like coaching and developing employees, creating strategic plans and solutions, and engaging and leading a team, feel less tangible. Staying in technical work feels more rewarding because we get the immediate satisfaction from checking things off a list. Again, we often think the value we bring to the organization is our technical expertise, but frequently, that expertise is what holds us back. To be an exceptional leader, we need to focus on leading and influencing our team towards results through coaching, developing, and giving meaningful feedback.

To be effective, leaders need to act as facilitators, not fixers. Your role isn't to dive into the weeds and solve every technical issue, but to create the conditions that enable your team to perform at their best. Great leaders guide, support, and empower others to find solutions and deliver results.

That said, being a facilitator doesn't mean being hands-off. There are times when stepping into the trenches with your team is necessary, especially during high-pressure moments or when extra support is needed. But those moments should be the exception, not the norm. If you're always fixing, you're not leading. True leadership lies in developing your team to solve problems, take ownership, and deliver results without constant intervention.

You can't do everything on your own. Yet most of us were rewarded early in our careers for our individual contributions and technical expertise. So when we step into leadership, it's easy to believe that our personal talent will continue to sustain our success.

But leadership isn't about what *you* can do; it's about what you can help *others* do. Your role now is to shift the focus from your own performance to developing the performance of your team. Leadership requires a mindset shift from *me* to *we*—from doing the work to empowering others to succeed.

COMMON EXAMPLES THAT CONTRIBUTE TO A LACK OF DELEGATION

- Believing it's easier or faster to just do it yourself
- The need to be in control
- Micromanaging tasks instead of trusting your team
- Thinking there is only one right way to do things (your way!)
- Believing you have to do it all (which is impossible)
- Enjoying or getting satisfaction from technical work
- Thinking your value to the organization is your technical expertise (when you transition to a leadership position, your value is the leadership competencies, not technical competencies)
- Feeling guilty about assigning work to others
- Not taking the time to train or explain expectations clearly

- Holding onto responsibilities outside of your Key Result Areas
- Confusing delegation with dumping or giving up responsibility
- Fearing that others will make mistakes or fall short
- Assuming your team doesn't want more responsibility
- Seeing delegation as a weakness rather than a leadership strength

In my example at the beginning of this chapter, I was not only ineffective at delegating responsibility, but I also didn't realize how essential it was for my success. The feedback Deb gave me was an important first step in getting me focused on the right areas as a leader, but it took time for me to develop the skill of delegation. I struggled not only to shift out of the technical, but I often found myself fixing issues for my staff instead of empowering them to handle challenges on their own. I was so busy doing, I had no time for meaningful coaching sessions or development with my team, or any margin in my schedule for planning and strategic thinking. I was constantly overwhelmed and kept getting in my own way. I had to consciously work on not getting pulled into the weeds and instead shifting tasks that weren't a good use of my time to my team.

> WHEN YOU DELEGATE, YOU MULTIPLY YOUR PRODUCTIVITY, AND YOU DEVELOP OTHERS ON YOUR TEAM.

When you delegate, you multiply your productivity, *and* you develop others on your team. To make the successful transition to leadership, managers have to let go of being the technical expert and shift into a facilitator role, which will enable their team to grow and perform at their best.

5. CONFLICT AVOIDANT

Leaders with the Conflict Avoidant saboteur tend to prioritize keeping the peace, often at the expense of addressing important issues directly. This avoidance often stems from fear—whether it's fear of conflict, discomfort with difficult conversations, or worry about straining relationships. As a result, difficult conversations about poor performance, unmet expectations, or interpersonal tension are delayed or ignored.

While avoidance may seem like a way to preserve harmony, it ultimately has the opposite effect over time. It erodes trust, creates lingering tension, and weakens morale. Employees can feel overlooked, unsupported, or frustrated when issues are swept under the rug. Ultimately, conflict-avoidant leaders lose credibility and miss critical opportunities to coach, realign, and strengthen their teams. Leadership is not about avoiding discomfort; it's about facing it with clarity, empathy, and courage.

Leaders who fall into the trap of the Conflict Avoidant saboteur often struggle with striking the right balance between maintaining a positive, collaborative atmosphere and taking necessary, sometimes uncomfortable, actions to resolve issues. Without addressing underlying problems, these issues can fester, leading to further disengagement and a lack of alignment within the team.

COMMON EXAMPLES THAT CONTRIBUTE TO CONFLICT AVOIDANCE

- Avoiding conversations about poor performance
- Hoping problems will resolve themselves without intervention
- Delaying difficult feedback until it becomes urgent
- Sugarcoating or minimizing the real issue
- Prioritizing short-term comfort over long-term results
- Worrying too much about being liked
- Believing conflict will permanently damage relationships

- Letting frustrations build up instead of addressing them early
- Failing to establish clear expectations from the start
- Confusing kindness with passivity

6. PASSIVE APPROACH

In more traditional work environments, managers could often be successful by reacting to problems as they arose. They waited for issues to come to them, stepped in when needed, and focused primarily on maintaining output. But today's workplace requires a very different approach. Modern leadership demands daily engagement. Managers must actively lead through team meetings, alignment conversations, coaching, feedback, removing roadblocks, and building connections.

It's easier to stay in your office, answer emails, or focus on independent tasks than to initiate difficult conversations, schedule one-on-ones, or engage in coaching. But leadership isn't about convenience, it's about presence and intentionality. And in today's workplace, that's even more challenging. Many managers now lead hybrid teams, with some employees working remotely and others on site. Leading people you don't see every day takes more energy, effort, and follow-through. It requires a proactive approach to communication, relationship-building, and accountability.

True leadership is not about stepping in occasionally or reacting only when problems arise. It is a daily commitment to stay engaged, communicate clearly, and build a culture of trust and accountability. Leaders with the Passive Approach saboteur often underestimate what leadership truly requires, or they lack the training, confidence, or clarity to lead proactively. Instead of providing direction, support, and feedback consistently, they remain on the sidelines, hoping things will work themselves out.

Passive leaders may not intend to disengage. In many cases, they are trying to avoid micromanaging, or they are so caught up in technical tasks that leadership work takes a back seat. But in doing so, they leave their team without the clarity, guidance, and recognition they need to thrive. Over time, this hands-off approach leads to confusion, missed opportunities, and a team that feels unsupported.

In today's evolving workplace, leadership cannot be reactive or invisible. It must be intentional, consistent, and centered on people—no matter where or how they work.

COMMON EXAMPLES THAT CONTRIBUTE TO A PASSIVE APPROACH

- Failing to set clear expectations or goals for the team
- Avoiding feedback conversations because they feel uncomfortable
- Rarely checking in with employees or having one-on-one conversations
- Not recognizing or appreciating employee contributions
- Letting team dynamics or issues go unaddressed
- Assuming people know what is expected without confirming
- Getting caught up in technical tasks instead of leading
- Responding to issues only when they escalate
- Believing that being hands-off is the same as being empowering
- Lacking a consistent leadership presence or message
- Failing to realign the team around changing priorities

At the core of the Six Leadership Saboteurs is a persistent overemphasis on technical tasks, a focus that prevents leaders from stepping into the broader responsibilities of leadership. All six saboteurs can stem from spending too much time in the weeds of technical work, neglecting the essential leadership competencies that create success.

For example, when leaders fail to focus on the most critical aspects of leadership, such as coaching, communication, and delegation, they often find themselves without the capacity to truly engage and support their team. Likewise, a lack of self-awareness can lead to disengagement by creating blind spots around how one's behavior affects others. Leadership isn't just a step up from technical expertise; it requires a complete shift in mindset and behavior. It demands energy, focus, and intention to move from being a skilled individual contributor to becoming an effective, empowering leader.

To thrive in today's workplace, leaders must step into the role of facilitators, not fixers. Rather than operating on autopilot, this is an opportunity to lead with greater clarity, intention, and purpose, focusing on what truly enhances performance, culture, and growth.

The good news is, this shift is entirely possible. The mindset and skills needed to lead at a higher level and build a thriving team can be developed with intention and practice. My goal is to walk alongside you as a guide and coach, helping you recognize and overcome the habits that may be holding you back. In the chapters ahead, I'll show you where to focus your time, energy, and attention so you can lead a more engaged, empowered team, while reducing the stress and pressure that so often come with managing people.

PART 2

THE INNER WORK OF ELEVATED LEADERSHIP

4

THE ELEVATED LEADER MODEL

[Strategy] is more than a science: it is the application of
knowledge to practical life, the development of thought
capable of modifying the original guiding idea in the light
of ever-changing situations; it is the art of acting under
the pressure of the most difficult conditions.

—Helmuth Von Moltke

Up to this point, we've explored the evolving demands of leadership; how the workplace has changed, why traditional management approaches fall short, and what it truly takes to lead with impact today. You've seen how common leadership pitfalls, or saboteurs, can limit effectiveness and erode team culture. Now, I'll introduce a framework that brings the essential principles of effective leadership into focus and shows you how to integrate them to lead with greater intention and impact.

The Elevated Leader model offers a clear, practical framework for developing the mindset, habits, and skills modern leaders need to succeed. Built on a foundation of well-being and intention, this model integrates both the internal and external elements of leadership to help you approach your role with clarity, lead with purpose, and elevate the performance of both yourself and your team.

The model emphasizes that a leader's internal landscape—beliefs, mindset, strengths, and personal practices—directly shapes their external leadership effectiveness. True leadership isn't just about your actions; it's about the mindset and intention behind them. It highlights the importance of cultivating high energy through personal vitality and mental resilience. Self-awareness is developed through consistent reflection and a deep understanding of one's strengths, limitations, and impact on others. Reflection becomes a regular discipline, enabling leaders to learn from experiences, adapt, find space for strategic thinking, and continuously evolve.

Externally, the Elevated Leader model is built upon the pillars of creating clarity, caretaking the culture, and facilitating results. Leaders create clarity by articulating a clear vision, setting transparent goals, and providing direction that inspires and aligns teams toward a common purpose. Caretaking the culture involves actively shaping an environment of trust, collaboration, and innovation, ensuring a positive and supportive workplace that nurtures individual growth and collective success.

In addition, leaders who embrace this model consistently facilitate results by using coaching strategies, involving team members in meaningful decisions, and offering timely, constructive feedback. This approach empowers individuals, promotes accountability, and facilitates sustainable, measurable outcomes.

The Elevated Leader model supports a holistic leadership approach that prioritizes both personal and organizational well-being while integrating intention, energy, self-awareness, reflection, clarity creation, culture caretaking, and results to foster impactful and transformative leadership that influences others in a positive, respectful, and effective way.

This model aligns with effective modern leadership practices that prioritize a relational leadership style over the traditional transactional leadership style.

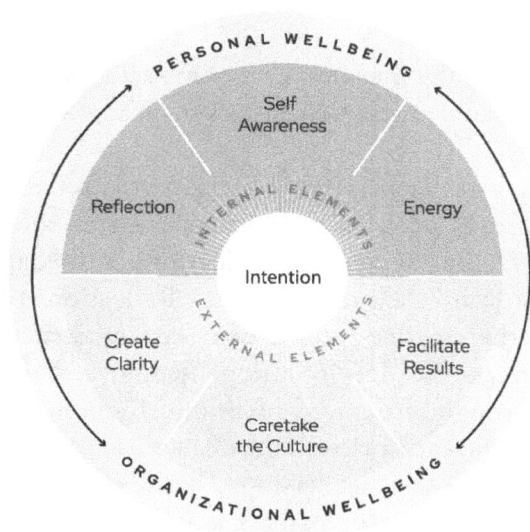

Well-Being: Well-being surrounds the model as the foundational and encompassing element forming the outermost ring. It represents the overarching philosophy of an Elevated Leader that both personal and organizational health are the cornerstones of a thriving team and culture. It embodies the collective essence of a leader's focus, representing both personal and organizational vitality, resilience, and health. It acknowledges that employees are human beings who crave work that is personally fulfilling and contributes positively to their personal lives.

Intention: Intention forms the core of the Elevated Leader model, signifying the importance of purposeful leadership. It embodies a deliberate approach, infusing every interaction and moment mindfully. Elevated Leaders navigate their day with a focused intent, characterized by reflective pauses that empower them to respond thoughtfully rather than react impulsively. This intentional approach extends to how they allocate their time, channel their energy, and make decisive, intentional choices, fostering a leadership style that is deliberate, impactful, and deeply aligned with their vision and values.

INTERNAL ELEMENTS

The top segment of the Elevated Leader model is dedicated to internal focus, an essential aspect that fosters the leader's personal growth and effectiveness.

Reflection: An essential tool for growth, reflection encourages leaders to introspect, learn from experiences, and refine their approaches. It facilitates continuous learning and adaptation, propelling leaders toward their full potential. Reflection is also a crucial component in the creative process of designing a successful vision and strategy. Effective leaders intentionally build reflection into their daily work—through structured planning, thoughtful pauses, and regular evaluation of priorities and decisions—creating space for more intentional, strategic leadership. They also meet regularly with their teams to reflect on progress, assess what's working, and adjust course as needed. Great leaders skillfully shift perspectives, zooming out to plan with foresight while zooming in to support day-to-day execution that aligns with long-term goals.

Self-Awareness: Foundational to effective leadership, self-awareness involves a deep understanding of one's strengths, weaknesses, emotions, and impact on others. It fosters authenticity and guides decision-making with clarity. Self-awareness also includes the emotional intelligence required for leaders to navigate challenges, adeptly guide individuals through continuous change, and navigate challenging conversations and situations.

Energy: This vital component centers on cultivating high levels of personal vitality and mental resilience. It encompasses practices that optimize physical, mental, and emotional energy to sustain peak performance, motivation, and initiative. This element also reflects the positive energy required to build, sustain, and effectively inspire and manage a thriving team.

This internal focus within the Elevated Leader model nurtures a leader's inner mindset, empowering them to harness their energy, deepen self-understanding, and evolve through continuous introspection and learning, thereby enhancing their leadership capacity.

EXTERNAL ELEMENTS

The bottom segment of the Elevated Leader model is dedicated to the external focus, representing the leader's outward actions and influence within their team and organization.

Create Clarity: An essential element of effective leadership is the ability to articulate a clear vision, set specific goals, and communicate direction. Leaders adept at creating clarity provide a roadmap that inspires and aligns their teams toward a shared purpose and vision. In addition, leaders must foster clarity for themselves by prioritizing their Key Result Areas, allowing them to concentrate on the pivotal elements crucial for achieving leadership success.

Caretake the Culture: Cultivating a positive and supportive workplace culture is a hallmark of an Elevated Leader. Managers proactively foster an atmosphere rooted in trust, collaboration, and innovation. By championing diversity, inclusivity, and continuous growth, these leaders empower individuals to flourish and make meaningful contributions. They achieve this by forging connections, offering constructive feedback, proactively coaching and developing each individual, and fostering a positive and productive team environment. Managers also encourage constructive conflict within the team, valuing diverse perspectives and fostering healthy debates that lead to innovative solutions. Moreover, when necessary for the team's benefit, they take decisive action to address underperformance, ensuring the team's overall success and well-being.

Facilitate Results: An Elevated Leader adeptly facilitates results through coaching, engaging team members in decision-making processes, and offering valuable feedback. Managers model and instill accountability in a positive, respectful manner, nurturing a culture that values responsibility and celebrates achievements. They remove roadblocks, delegate appropriately, stay attuned to priorities, and make timely, thoughtful decisions. By aligning goals and strategies, Elevated Leaders proactively anticipate challenges and guide their teams toward success. They empower their teams to excel, facilitating collective efforts toward measurable outcomes while fostering a culture of accountability and achievement.

This external focus within the Elevated Leader model signifies the leader's ability to guide, inspire, and facilitate impactful change within their organization by providing direction, fostering a nurturing culture, and enabling their teams to achieve tangible results aligned with the broader vision.

Now that you've delved into the foundational principles of the Elevated Leader model, this book will guide you on a transformative journey. Throughout its pages, we'll explore each element of this model, offering insights and strategies to not only elevate your leadership but also enrich your life.

5

INTENTION

*Intentional living is the art of making our
own choices before others' choices make us.*

—Richie Norton

Jen, a mid-level manager in a fast-growing financial institution, had a habit of starting her day by immediately diving into her overflowing inbox. Each morning, she would spend the first hour of her day responding to emails, attending to urgent requests, and putting out fires that had emerged overnight. This reactive approach left her feeling constantly frazzled and overwhelmed, as she struggled to keep up with the demands of her role.

Despite her best intentions to set priorities and focus on strategic tasks, Jen found herself constantly pulled in different directions by the demands of others. She often stayed late at the office, trying to catch up on important projects that had been pushed aside in favor of more immediate tasks.

Over time, Jen began to realize that her lack of intention at the start of her day was taking a toll on her well-being and effectiveness as a leader. She decided to make a change and enrolled in a leadership coaching program. Over the next several months, Jen started to reclaim her leadership influence. She ended each day by setting aside 10 minutes to plan for the following day. During this time, she would review her priorities, identify the most important tasks for the day, and set clear goals for what she wanted to accomplish. She also implemented several other powerful strategies, such as productivity sprints, priority planning, and the Five Minutes to Clarity Method, all of which we will explore in this book.

By starting her day with intention, Jen found that she was able to approach her work with greater focus and clarity. She was better able to prioritize her tasks, delegate effectively, and avoid getting caught up in the cycle of reacting to urgent but unimportant demands. As a result, Jen felt more in control of her time and more empowered in her role as a leader.

TRAPPED IN THE MESSY MIDDLE

Jen's experience is far from unique; it highlights a broader challenge faced by countless middle managers navigating what I call the *messy middle*. It's a demanding space where leaders must bridge the gap between executing the vision of senior leadership and meeting the day-to-day needs of their teams through management, development, and support.

What makes the messy middle even more difficult is the outdated model of the "working manager"—where managers are expected to perform technical, individual-contributor tasks while also carrying the full weight of leadership. While this approach may have been effective in the past, when leadership was more transactional and focused on oversight and problem-solving, it no longer aligns with the demands of today's workplace. Modern leadership requires emotional intelligence, strategic thinking, and dedicated time to build culture, coach employees, and lead with intention. Yet many organizations still operate with this outdated expectation, making it nearly impossible for managers to be effective in both roles.

The reality is, today's model of the working manager is placing an unsustainable burden on middle managers. They're expected to lead teams and execute technical work simultaneously—often without the time, support, or training to lead effectively. Research from McKinsey shows that middle managers spend only about 28 percent of their time on people development and team management, while the majority is consumed by meetings, administrative tasks, and technical responsibilities.[5] These are not the activities that cultivate high-performing teams or elevate culture.

To make matters worse, many organizations set ambitious strategic priorities without thoroughly evaluating whether the necessary resources, time, and staffing are in place to support them. This disconnect between goals and capacity creates a cycle of unrealistic expectations, reactive management, and burnout. Managers often aren't overwhelmed because they lack motivation; they're overwhelmed because they lack the structure, support, and clarity needed to prioritize what matters most.

While these systemic challenges are real, they don't have to define your experience as a leader. Despite the time pressure and competing demands, there are strategies that can help you lead with more clarity, confidence, and impact. One of the most powerful is intention.

Leading with intention means choosing how you spend your time and energy rather than defaulting to the urgent and reactive. It means aligning your focus with what matters most—your people, your team culture, and your results. When intention becomes a consistent practice, even in small ways, it can help you move from survival mode to strategic leadership. In today's environment, leadership demands more, but with the right tools and mindset, you can rise to meet it.

THE POWER OF INTENTIONALITY

Intention is the foundation of effective leadership and the core of The Elevated Leader model. Leadership is not just about what you do, but why and how you do it. Purposeful actions and deliberate energy set the tone for team culture, facilitate results, and inspire excellence. Leaders who act with intention create clarity, foster accountability, and make a lasting impact.

Intentionality manifests in various forms: in how you approach each day, in the strategic decisions you make as a leader, how you respond to conflict and difficult situations, and in the mindful choices you embrace in your life.

Through more than 20 years of leadership and team development experience, I've seen many patterns that undermine leadership effectiveness, but one of the most common and costly is the struggle to focus on what matters most. Too many leaders are stuck in a cycle of back-to-back meetings, reactive problem-solving, and endless to-do lists, leaving them overwhelmed and ineffective. This constant busyness, often praised or normalized within organizations, leaves leaders overwhelmed, distracted, and disconnected from the Key Result Areas that will create the most impactful results. Over time, it erodes not only their effectiveness but also their ability to lead with clarity and intention.

Effective leadership isn't about being busy—it's about managing energy, focus, and priorities with intention. While unpredictable days and challenges are inevitable, being overwhelmed shouldn't be the standard. Exceptional leaders are intentional with their time and energy, adapting to change while maintaining clarity and focus on what matters most.

In both leadership and life, adopting a mindset that centers on what you can influence is key to improving your outcomes. When you focus on what you can control—your actions, mindset, and approach—you create greater agency over your circumstances. While your manager and organizational culture can certainly impact your time and focus, you have the greatest power to shape how you spend them. If you believe external factors completely dictate your time and energy, you may struggle to lead effectively.

A few years ago, I read an impactful book called *Do the Work* by Steven Pressfield, which shifted my perspective on how I approach my work, leadership, and life.[6] Pressfield discusses the difference between amateurs and professionals through the lens of writing, emphasizing that amateurs dabble—waiting for inspiration, making excuses, and avoiding the hard work—while professionals approach their craft with consistency, discipline, and intention. The concept of moving from amateur to professional immediately resonated with me, not just as a personal philosophy but as a powerful framework for leadership. Pressfield describes the pivotal moment when we stop dabbling, making excuses, or waiting for the "right time" and instead commit fully to our craft. It's the shift from passively going through the motions to actively stepping up with discipline, ownership, and a higher standard.

As leaders, we must make the crucial shift from amateur to professional, approaching leadership with intention, discipline, and a commitment to continuous growth, just as any elite performer hones their craft with focus and rigor. Too many leaders operate as amateurs: reactive, unintentional, and unprepared for the true demands of the role.

The Elevated Leader model centers on this principle: leaders who master intentionality elevate their influence, inspire their teams, and achieve impactful results. This model helps leaders make the crucial shift from amateur to professional by emphasizing consistent focus, discipline, and ownership. Regardless of talent or expertise, leaders cannot succeed without effectively managing both their own energy and that of their teams.

Amateurs complain, blame, and look outside themselves for why they can't focus on the right things. They fail to see the importance of taking ownership, allowing distractions and external factors to dictate their effectiveness. Professionals, on the other hand, intentionally implement structures that support their success: closing email, reducing distractions, and creating an environment where they can maintain their best focus.

We all know that if you want to lose weight and get healthier, the best chance at success is to set up your environment to support you. If your challenge is avoiding junk food or chocolate, the first step is to remove those temptations so they're not within easy reach. You become intentional with meal planning, stocking up on healthy snacks, and structuring your day to set yourself up for success. Without that preparation, the moment stress hits, you'll default to old habits, grabbing the chocolate instead of making a better choice.

The same principle applies to how we manage our day. Most people don't set up their environment to support their best focus. Instead, they leave distractions wide open: email notifications pinging, multiple browser tabs cluttering their screen, and no clear plan for their priorities. Just like with healthy habits, if we don't proactively structure our environment for success, we'll inevitably fall into reactive, unproductive patterns.

That is the power of intentionality.

Imagine leading with clarity, purpose, and impact every day. You come to work energized, pursue progress toward organizational goals, and dedicate time to what matters: coaching, feedback, and developing your team. Under your guidance, your team thrives, and you end each day with a sense of accomplishment and impact. This vision is achievable.

Protecting your energy and focus is essential for leadership success.

Cultivating Intention Into Your Life

In his remarks at the National Defense Executive Reserve Conference in 1957, President Dwight Eisenhower shared a quote that he had learned in the Army: "Plans are worthless, but planning is everything."[7]

What Eisenhower is suggesting is not that planning is a waste of time, but that the true value lies in the process of thinking through possibilities, priorities, and contingencies, not in the plan itself. In leadership, just like in military strategy, the environment is constantly shifting. Circumstances change, new information emerges, and unexpected challenges arise. But when leaders engage deeply in the act of planning, they build clarity, foresight, and adaptability, tools that equip them to pivot effectively when the situation demands it. The planning process helps leaders and teams align on what matters most, consider various outcomes, and prepare mentally for change. It's not about rigidly sticking to the plan; it's about building the strategic muscle to adjust with intention when the plan no longer fits.

Even something as simple as planning your day can lead to increased focus, better decision-making, and improved outcomes. It doesn't guarantee that everything will go according to plan, but it gives structure to your time and helps you respond rather than react. The act of planning itself builds the foundation for more intentional leadership.

Part of the reason planning is so powerful is that it helps manage stress—something every leader experiences. While stress often has a negative connotation, not all stress is harmful. In 1974, Hungarian endocrinologist Hans Selye introduced the concept of two types of stress: *eustress* (positive stress) and *distress* (negative stress).[8] Eustress is the kind that pushes us to grow, learn new skills, and rise to challenges. It's the healthy pressure that fuels momentum and achievement.

On the other hand, distress arises from chronic overwhelm— long hours, constant interruptions, excessive workloads, ineffective meetings, and lack of clarity. Left unmanaged, it leads to burnout, disengagement, and poor performance.

Intentional planning helps mitigate distress by giving you more control over your day, helping you focus on what matters most, and creating mental space to respond thoughtfully. When we build daily habits that bring structure, clarity, and focus, we reduce unnecessary stress and increase our capacity to lead with purpose and resilience, even in the face of uncertainty.

We will explore more planning and productivity strategies in the Creating Clarity section of this book, but here are three practices and habits that can support leading with intention.

1. **Plan your next day before you leave the office.** Set aside 10 minutes at the end of your workday to reflect on what you've accomplished and identify the two most important tasks or projects to prioritize for tomorrow. Planning your day in advance helps eliminate decision fatigue and allows you to start with clarity and focus. Personally, I find planning to be one of the most effective ways to relieve stress. When I feel overwhelmed, taking a moment to pause, reset, and create a plan almost always helps me feel more grounded and in control.

2. **Make an intention** before starting your day and each time you switch to something new. For example:

   a. When you start work, make an intention about the next hour: "I will turn off distractions and completely focus on this project for one hour."

    b. Make an intention before each meeting: "I will take these 10 minutes to prepare for my meeting and be completely present and focused on my colleagues."

    c. Before lunch, "I will leave my office and disconnect from work for 30 minutes."

    d. Before ending your day, "I will stop work at 5:30 and be ready to greet my children with enthusiasm when they walk through the door."

3. **Instill clear boundaries.** Establishing clear boundaries is crucial for effective leadership. By setting boundaries around your availability and workload, you can avoid distractions and maintain focus on important objectives. Clear boundaries also help prevent burnout by allowing you to manage your workload and schedule in a sustainable way. By setting limits on working hours and taking regular breaks, you can maintain your well-being and effectiveness. We will explore boundaries in a future chapter.

Intentionally Navigating Relationships

Just as intentional planning helps us manage our time and energy, bringing that same level of intention to our relationships allows us to lead with greater emotional intelligence, especially under pressure.

In times of stress, many of us tend to react impulsively rather than taking a moment to respond thoughtfully. The ability to pause is one of the most underrated skills in both leadership and life. By taking a moment to pause in times of stress or uncertainty, we can cultivate more purposeful responses.

When we engage with others intentionally, we build stronger relationships, reduce unnecessary conflict, and navigate disagreements with greater emotional intelligence. This intentionality fosters a healthier team environment; one where conflict is constructive rather than destructive, and where individuals feel seen, supported, and respected.

It also allows us to respond from our most grounded, thoughtful self instead of reacting from a place of frustration or defensiveness. In my work as a leadership consultant, I frequently see teams struggle with dynamics driven by differing personalities, values, and communication styles. While healthy conflict can drive innovation and growth, unmanaged tension, backchanneling, and blame-shifting drain energy and erode trust, ultimately weakening collaboration and performance.

Elevated leaders consciously engage in every individual and team interaction with a mindset of listening, curiosity, and patience. They nurture a style of leadership that is both empathetic and empowering.

MODEL FOR INTENTIONAL INTERACTIONS

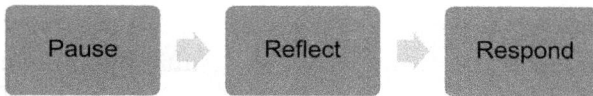

Pause ➔ Reflect ➔ Respond

Pause: Before reacting to a situation, take a moment to pause. This brief pause helps you step away from an immediate emotional response, creating space for a more thoughtful and deliberate reaction. Research shows that in stressful moments, emotions can hijack our rational thinking, making it harder to respond rationally.[9]

Reflect: Use this pause to reflect on the situation. Consider the perspectives of others involved, as well as your own feelings and motivations. Think about the outcome you want to achieve and how your actions can contribute to that outcome.

Respond: After pausing and reflecting, respond to the situation with intention. Choose your words and actions carefully, aiming to achieve the desired outcome while maintaining positive relationships and respect for others.

By embracing this model, you can approach interactions with greater mindfulness and purpose, fostering more effective communication and stronger relationships. However, in my experience, this is easier said than done. Responding with intention is a skill that requires practice and deliberate effort to master. In stressful situations, practice pausing and taking a moment to reflect or create space before responding. This allows you to approach the situation with clarity and intention rather than reacting impulsively.

Intention is the foundation of impactful leadership, guiding every action and decision with purpose and clarity. It sharpens focus and keeps you and your team aligned around organizational priorities. Intentional leaders inspire and influence by sharing a clear vision and by prioritizing the people on their team. Through intentionality, leaders not only elevate their own effectiveness but also empower their teams to thrive and achieve meaningful goals.

While no day is perfect, intentional leadership transforms your influence, reduces stress, and amplifies results. By implementing the principles in this book, you will elevate your leadership effectiveness, create a lasting impact, and foster a culture of success within your team and organization.

When you develop a mindset of intention, you accelerate your results, preserve your well-being, cultivate thriving teams, and foster fulfillment for both you and your team.

6

WELL-BEING

Well-being is realized by small steps,
but is truly no small thing.

—Zeno, Quoted in *Lives and Opinions of*
Eminent Philosophers by Diogenes Laertius

For years, leadership has been defined by hustle—by pushing harder, doing more, and measuring success through output and hours. But sustainable leadership requires something deeper. It's not just about delivering results; it's about leading in a way that supports both high performance and personal well-being.

When I started my business in 2008, I was driven by big dreams, clear ambition, and a deep desire to make an impact. I knew building a business would take focus and relentless effort, but I also knew one thing for sure: I didn't want success to come at the cost of my personal life. From the very beginning, I was intentional about finding better, smarter ways to work—approaches that allowed me to grow my business while still being present for my life. Over the past 17 years, I have been on a continuous quest to find better, smarter ways to work—ones that allow me to achieve my business goals and enjoy my life.

What I've learned on that journey is this: the same principles that support a fulfilling life are also the foundation of effective leadership. Many leaders start out energized and ambitious, but quickly get swept into a culture that equates overwork with dedication. Long hours, packed calendars, and constant urgency are worn like badges of honor. Yet beneath the surface, many of these leaders are burned out, disconnected, and running on empty.

This way of working is not sustainable, and it's not effective leadership. Great leadership is about creating a rhythm that sustains both performance and well-being. It means managing with clarity, intention, and energy, and creating an environment where people feel supported, coached, and valued.

> Well-being: a state of being comfortable, healthy, and happy.[10]

Well-being is no longer optional; it is a core element of strong leadership and sustainable organizational success. In today's workplace, employees need more than a paycheck and a job description; they need to feel supported, connected, and valued. Well-being reflects positive functioning: when people experience psychological safety, support, and a sense of purpose, they are more focused, energized, and able to contribute at their highest level.

Effective well-being isn't driven by perks or wellness programs alone; it's embedded in the daily leadership behaviors that shape the work experience. When managers hold regular check-ins, set clear expectations, provide thoughtful coaching, and lead with empathy and respect, they cultivate environments where people can thrive. In contrast, toxic or overly demanding managers who lack emotional intelligence can undermine well-being, fueling stress, burnout, and disengagement—even in high-performing organizations.

That's why well-being forms the outer circle of The Elevated Leader model. It surrounds and reinforces every other leadership element. It reflects the belief that both personal and cultural well-being are essential for positive functioning, high performance, and long-term engagement. Leaders who prioritize well-being don't just improve team outcomes; they create workplaces where people flourish.

There are two key elements of well-being: **personal** and **organizational**.

PERSONAL WELL-BEING

Personal well-being encompasses the flexibility and freedom to enjoy life outside of work, including healthy boundaries, meaningful family time, opportunities to rest and recharge, and the ability to fully engage in life beyond professional responsibilities. Organizations that expect constant availability, overlook work-life balance, and prioritize short-term results over employee well-being will ultimately struggle to sustain long-term success.

Today's employees are no longer willing to sacrifice their personal lives for a job that drains them. They seek work that supports and enhances their well-being, led by leaders who recognize and appreciate their contributions. To build an exceptional culture, organizations must move beyond productivity metrics and focus on what truly drives success: leaders who prioritize both personal and organizational well-being, knowing that the manager-employee relationship is the most critical factor in workplace fulfillment.

Our personal well-being directly influences our work, relationships, and overall life satisfaction. Yet, despite all the advancements and comforts of modern life, rates of depression and anxiety are higher than ever. The United States ranks among the most anxious and depressed countries, with rising addiction rates and a growing sense of disconnection. The World Health Organization reported a **25 percent increase** in depression and anxiety in just the first year of the COVID-19 pandemic.[11] Dr. John Delony, a mental health and wellness expert, explains that anxiety isn't a disease but rather our body's way of signaling distress. He emphasizes that a *non-anxious life* is one where we pause, listen to these internal alarms, and take control of what we can—our thoughts, behaviors, and choices.[12] It requires the courage to step back, be intentional, and choose peace over relentless striving.

Most people today live in a constant state of stress, running on empty, with their well-being and health suffering as a result. But success shouldn't come at the cost of personal fulfillment. The key is working with clarity and intention—maximizing impact while maintaining balance.

While company executives shape workplace culture, *your* daily choices influence your well-being and productivity. By implementing intentional practices, you can achieve more in less time, without sacrificing your health, energy, or personal life.

BOUNDARIES ELEVATE FOCUS, PRODUCTIVITY, AND PEAK PERFORMANCE

The word "boundaries" often makes people uneasy, as it can feel like we're creating barriers or being selfish—choosing ourselves at the expense of others. But boundaries aren't about exclusion or control; they're about creating the structure we need to operate at our best. While they may affect others, boundaries are ultimately for you—helping you manage your energy, maintain focus, and protect your well-being so you can lead and live with greater impact.

Healthy boundaries provide the clarity and space needed to thrive. They enhance productivity, define roles and expectations, and strengthen relationships by fostering mutual respect and open communication. Boundaries aren't about shutting others out; they're about creating the conditions that allow you to lead and work at your best. While occasional emergencies are inevitable, operating in constant crisis mode should not be the norm. Boundaries create the structure leaders need to stay focused, think strategically, and maintain well-being for themselves and their teams.

Personal boundaries are intentional decisions that protect your time, energy, and focus, allowing you to lead and live with purpose. They serve as internal guardrails, helping you stay aligned with your values, honor your priorities, and operate at your best.

For example, in my household, we stick to a consistent bedtime during the week. I deeply value sleep, and I've learned over time that when we are all well-rested, everything functions better—mornings are smoother, we're more patient with each other, and we have the energy for the day ahead. This boundary may seem simple, but it has a big impact on our overall well-being and the tone of our home. It's one of the ways I protect not just my own energy, but also support the well-being and functioning of our entire family.

Examples of Work Boundaries

- Fully disconnecting from work during evenings, weekends, and vacations
- Avoiding emails outside of core work hours
- Creating team agreements on how to manage interruptions
- Clarifying which communication channels to use for different needs
- (e.g., Teams for quick chats, email for formal updates, text for urgent matters)
- Communicating when you need uninterrupted focus time, such as by closing your door and setting expectations of when you will be available
- Working from a conference room or quiet space to concentrate on deep work
- Establishing regular "office hours" so team members know when they can access your support
- Closing your email or silencing notifications during focused tasks
- Compressing your schedule instead of extending your workday or workweek
- Physically closing your home office door at the end of the day to reinforce work-life boundaries

Examples of Personal Boundaries

- Prioritizing sleep with a consistent bedtime on weeknights
- Avoiding screen time, such as TV, before bed on weeknights to support better rest
- Charging your phone outside the bedroom to minimize distractions
- Limiting caffeine or alcohol intake (for me, this is no more than one glass of wine on weekdays)

- Scheduling regular physical activity, for example, 4–5 walks each week
- Setting a firm end to the workday, such as leaving the office by 5:30 PM
- Fully unplugging from work on weekends and vacations
- Limiting weekend commitments (for me, this is no more than one night out per weekend to preserve my energy)

Our daily practices support our focus, results, and growth so that we can be at our best every day and effectively serve those whom we lead.

About eight years ago, I made a non-negotiable rule for myself: when I'm on vacation, I fully disconnect. Before that, I checked my email every day to stay ahead of the inbox, but the result was a low (and sometimes high) level of anxiety the entire vacation. Even benign messages kept my brain thinking about work, and I never truly rested. I hear from many managers and executives who stay connected during their vacations, and I believe this is a big mistake. Setting a firm boundary to unplug isn't indulgent; it's smart leadership. It models sustainability for your team, protects your energy, and ensures you return with clarity and capacity instead of depletion. If you typically don't disconnect when you go on vacation, I encourage you to try it. It may take a couple of days to truly relax, but I promise you'll experience a level of presence, rest, and enjoyment in your time away that you've likely never felt before.

If you're in the middle of a major project or there's a genuine reason your team might need your input, assign a point person who can be your single contact. That way, they can reach out only if something truly urgent comes up. For example, during my vacation in Maine this summer, we had key elements of our book launch in motion. My team member, Jalene, knew she could text me with any pressing questions or issues. This allowed me to stay out of my inbox while still ensuring the team had a direct line to me for anything essential.

If you find it hard to fully unwind and relax, as many high achievers do, try logging out of email on your phone during evenings and weekends. Your mind needs space to recharge, process, and shift out of work mode so you can return with fresh energy and perspective. I personally find that my best ideas rarely appear when I'm buried in day-to-day tasks; they come when I'm fully disconnected from the daily work. Stepping away creates the mental space for fresh perspectives, creative solutions, and strategic thinking to emerge. It's in those moments, whether on a walk, during a quiet morning, or while traveling, that the insights I couldn't force at my desk seem to arrive effortlessly. Disconnecting isn't just about rest; it's about giving your brain the freedom it needs to do its best work.

When you set and uphold boundaries—both at work and in your personal life—you create the conditions for sustained energy, focus, and high performance. Boundaries aren't about restriction; they're about intention. They allow you to lead with clarity, operate at your highest level, and cultivate a healthier, more productive environment for both you and your team.

ORGANIZATIONAL WELL-BEING

Organizational well-being reflects a culture where employees feel valued, supported, and fulfilled in their roles. It involves cultivating a positive work environment, offering meaningful responsibilities, providing opportunities for growth and development, supportive leadership and colleagues, and creating space for individuals to bring their authentic selves to work. One of the most influential factors in organizational well-being is the direct manager. A leader who builds trust, offers consistent coaching and feedback, and models healthy boundaries creates a space where employees can thrive. In contrast, a manager who micromanages, lacks empathy, or fails to invest in employee growth can diminish well-being, increase stress, and drive talent away.

Employees today seek more than just a paycheck; they want a career that enhances both their professional and personal well-being. The era of lifelong tenure at a single company, rewarded with a pension and a gold watch, is long gone. People are no longer willing to sacrifice their personal lives for relentless work hours. They want meaningful, fulfilling work that aligns with their well-being, alongside leaders who recognize, appreciate, and support their contributions. While this expectation may seem straightforward, creating a culture that truly nurtures both professional success and personal fulfillment is anything but simple.

Psychological safety is essential for a healthy work environment—employees need to feel valued, heard, and secure enough to speak up without fear. A toxic, demanding boss lacks the ability to truly listen and support their team, and erodes trust and well-being. While executives set the cultural tone, the direct manager has the greatest influence on how employees experience work. Your leadership shapes your team's engagement, job satisfaction, and overall well-being more than any policy or program ever could.

Strong leadership includes modeling boundaries, yet many managers struggle with this themselves. Even in organizations where top leaders encourage balance, some managers feel overwhelmed, unclear on priorities, and more focused on activities than results. These struggles aren't always obvious, but they directly impact their teams. A manager who lacks balance will inadvertently create an environment where burnout and disengagement thrive.

We'll explore strategies for enhancing organizational well-being in Chapter 12, but for now, these leadership practices will help you create an environment where employees feel valued, supported, and empowered to bring their best effort each day.

1. **Schedule Regular Check-Ins.** It's a simple yet often overlooked practice, but many leaders fail to hold consistent one-on-one meetings with their employees. These meetings provide a dedicated space for connection, feedback, and support while fostering engagement and alignment. When structured effectively, one-on-ones become a valuable opportunity to discuss updates, delegate responsibilities, offer coaching, and develop your team. Regular connection points not only strengthen relationships but also enhance productivity and morale.

2. **Model and Encourage Healthy Boundaries.** According to Parkinson's Law, work expands to fill the time available.[13] Successful leaders recognize that they can't do everything. The key is focusing on the highest-impact areas and ensuring their teams do the same. By setting and respecting boundaries, you model a culture of balance, allowing employees to recharge, maintain well-being, and bring their best energy to work each day.

3. **Prioritize Appreciation and Connection.** One of the top reasons employees leave their jobs is a lack of recognition for their contributions. Leadership is demanding, and balancing people and results can be challenging, but appreciation should never be an afterthought. Creating a culture of well-being and engagement starts with intentional, meaningful recognition. Whether it's a handwritten note, a small but thoughtful gift, or quality time spent with your team, simple acts of appreciation have a profound impact on morale, motivation, and retention.

Well-being isn't a perk—it must be a leadership priority. To create an exceptional culture, leaders should care about the whole person, not just work performance, and prioritize personal and organizational well-being. Not only will you create a culture where employees bring their best energy, effort, and engagement to work each day, but your team will also achieve significant results.

7

REFLECTION—OVERCOMING THE BUSYNESS TRAP

*I closed my eyes to look inward and
found a universe waiting to be explored.*

—Yung Pueblo

For many leaders, the day begins with the best intentions but quickly spirals into a whirlwind of interruptions, urgent requests, and endless busyness. Before you know it, the hours have slipped away, with half-finished tasks piling up and a lingering sense that you didn't accomplish anything meaningful. You work hard all day, yet leave the office feeling tired and frustrated, knowing you never got to your most important priorities.

Despite growing awareness of well-being and mental health in the workplace, many leaders and organizations remain caught in a culture that glorifies hustle and long hours. But true productivity doesn't come from constant activity; it comes from focusing on what matters most. Making time to reflect, plan, and think strategically is not a luxury; it's a leadership necessity.

I've built reflection into my leadership practices for years, but I'll be honest, it can still be challenging. Even with the best intentions, I find myself pulled into the urgency of the day. And if I waited to "find time" to reflect or work on strategic projects, it would never happen. There's always another meeting, another email, another issue to solve. That's why I've learned I need to intentionally create time for reflection. I need systems that support it, whether that's blocking time on my calendar, stepping away from my usual environment (I get my best ideas when I go for a walk), or holding regular strategy meetings with my team. Without these structures, it's easy to stay caught in low-value tasks and procrastinate on the focused thinking required to advance strategic projects that drive results and long-term success.

For most leaders, reflection feels like one more thing they just don't have time to squeeze in. They're caught in a reactive cycle, jumping from meeting to meeting, responding to emails, and putting out fires. But without stepping back to assess what's working and where to adjust, they risk staying busy without making real progress. Intentional leadership requires space to think, gain perspective, and make smarter decisions.

Reflection serves as the anchor that allows you to pause, assess, and strategically navigate the complexities of your role with purpose and foresight. In addition, self-reflection deepens your self-awareness, allowing you to identify your strengths and areas for growth, make more informed decisions, and make more intentional choices in both your personal and professional life.

KEY ELEMENTS OF REFLECTION IN LEADERSHIP

- **Self-Awareness:** Regularly assess your strengths, weaknesses, and behaviors to understand how they impact your leadership and team dynamics.
- **Alignment with Goals:** Evaluate whether your daily actions and decisions align with your team's and organization's long-term goals.
- **Strategic Thinking:** Step back to analyze challenges and opportunities from a broader perspective, ensuring thoughtful and effective decision-making.
- **Prioritization:** Reflect on current priorities to focus energy and resources on what will create the greatest impact.

> - **Learning from Experience:** Review past successes and setbacks to identify lessons and apply them to future situations.
> - **Team Awareness:** Consider the needs, dynamics, and performance of your team to provide better guidance, support, and motivation.

The ability to focus is one of the most essential leadership skills of our time. You can possess talent, empathy, strategic thinking skills, emotional intelligence, and self-awareness, but without the ability to channel your energy and focus into what truly matters, achieving meaningful results will always remain out of reach. Reflection plays a pivotal role in cultivating focus because it allows you to step back and evaluate your actions, decisions, and overall direction. By taking the time to reflect, you can identify what is working well and what needs improvement, enabling you to refocus on your priorities and align your actions with department and strategic goals.

Reflection also plays a crucial role in managing distractions by helping you regain clarity and focus. It allows you to pause and thoughtfully consider your responses rather than react impulsively, enabling more deliberate and effective decision-making. By taking time to reflect, you create space to evaluate your thoughts and emotions, which helps you choose more thoughtful responses in challenging situations.

STRATEGIC PLANNING

Reflection is a critical part of your growth as a leader and is essential for effective strategic planning. When you take the time to step back and reflect, you can make more thoughtful and effective decisions, ensuring your efforts are focused on what will create the greatest impact. Reflection helps you zoom out to see the bigger picture, aligning long-term goals with daily actions, and also zoom in to focus on the immediate priorities that matter most for you and your team. This practice allows you to think more creatively, explore innovative solutions, and move beyond simply checking off tasks. By creating space for this kind of intentional thinking, you strengthen your leadership, expand your influence, and build a solid foundation for long-term success.

In today's fast-paced and complex world, one of a leader's greatest responsibilities is staying in tune with what's happening within the organization and the broader environment, while continuously guiding the team in the right direction. With constant demands and shifting priorities, it's easy to get caught up in day-to-day tasks and lose sight of long-term goals. That's why making space for thoughtful reflection and intentional planning is essential. It allows you to step back, assess challenges and opportunities, and adjust your approach to keep your team aligned and focused. This deliberate pause not only sharpens your awareness of what your team needs but also empowers you to lead with clarity, purpose, and resilience in an ever-changing workplace.

Too many leaders consistently operate in reaction mode, consumed by daily tasks and interruptions, leaving little room for strategic thinking and planning. The truth is, breakthrough ideas don't emerge when you're stuck in the weeds of execution; they come when you step back, create mental space, and give yourself permission to think. To lead effectively, you must intentionally carve out time for strategy. Amateurs claim they're too busy for strategic thinking; professionals recognize it as an essential priority in their leadership.

Over seven years ago, I developed a personal practice of scheduling short retreats to step away from the daily demands of my business and focus on more strategic areas to move the business forward. In fact, most of this book was written during these retreats, which I increased to nearly monthly to accelerate progress. Taking just a few days to disconnect and clear my mind has proven invaluable—not only does it spark higher-quality ideas, but I always return feeling energized, motivated, and ready to implement. It's like a quick recharge that boosts my productivity and strategic focus.

Even a single day away from the office, whether spent at a coffee shop or in an inspiring setting, can provide the space to pause, reflect, and gain a fresh perspective. Stepping away from the daily demands allows you to return with greater clarity, renewed purpose, and the energy to tackle challenges with fresh insights. Leaders who don't intentionally carve out time for reflection miss out on its transformative power, leaving them stuck in reactivity rather than leading with vision and intention.

There are also ways you can build reflection practices into your everyday work. In my experience as a leadership consultant, the most successful managers and executives consistently implement foundational habits that support exceptional leadership; practices that many others mistakenly dismiss as too basic or not valuable. It's fairly simple to build time into your calendar, create space for priorities, and pause before you respond, but for most leaders, it's not easy. They undervalue these key foundational practices that can make all the difference in their success, in favor of the short-term satisfaction of handling interruptions and checking small tasks off their to-do list.

Failing to recognize the long-term consequences of short-term thinking is a key factor that undermines the performance of many leaders, preventing them from achieving sustained success. This limited perspective often leads to reactive decisions that prioritize immediate results over strategic planning, which can cause missed opportunities for growth, innovation, and team alignment. Leaders who embrace a broader, future-focused approach tend to make more thoughtful decisions that drive lasting impact and organizational success.

SIX WAYS TO INTEGRATE REFLECTION INTO YOUR LEADERSHIP

1. **Schedule regular reflection and planning time for you and your team.**

   - Block dedicated time on your calendar each week for uninterrupted planning. Use this time to evaluate progress, review decisions, and align your actions with your long-term goals.

- At the end of each day, review your priorities and tasks and reflect on the two most important priorities that need to be completed the next day. This sets you up to be more intentional with your focus the next morning.
- Schedule a monthly meeting with yourself to review strategic areas for your department and where your team needs to recalibrate. Go to a location where you won't be interrupted.
- Schedule a monthly strategic meeting with your team to review key strategic projects, discuss progress, and make any adjustments necessary to achieve results.

2. **Schedule personal and team retreats.**

- Every quarter, schedule personal and team time to completely disconnect from the office and discuss strategic progress, current challenges, industry changes, and future plans. Getting out of the office environment is crucial. You and your team will think more clearly and creatively when you are out of your typical workspace and in an environment with limited distractions and work. I recommend at least a half day for a retreat, but the more time you can dedicate, the better your results will be.

3. **Use purposeful pauses.**

- When facing a challenge, tough decision, or difficult conversation, take a moment to pause and reflect before responding. The purposeful pause can be one of your most powerful tools in leadership and life. Especially when emotions run high, taking time, whether it's a minute or a few days, before reacting allows you to respond from your most thoughtful and composed self, rather than out of frustration or anger.

4. **Prioritize leadership development.**

   o Self-awareness is a key element of successful lead-
     ership. Regularly meeting with industry colleagues,
     attending events, and participating in leadership
     development conferences and programs provides a
     space and platform for deeper reflection and idea
     exchanges, building your self-awareness so you can
     continuously elevate your leadership skills, influence,
     and impact.

5. **Implement an individual and team mid-year check-in.**

   o Taking time to intentionally review what is work-
     ing well and what isn't allows you and your team
     to recalibrate, adjust, and enhance relationships so
     you can accelerate performance. These questions are
     an effective framework for guiding the discussion:

     • What is working well on the team?
     • In what two areas do you feel the team has made
       the most significant progress or development
       this year?
     • What is not working well?
     • What are the top two potential challenges that
       could slow down success or results?
     • What two adjustments would have the biggest
       positive impact on our results this year?

6. **Disconnect from work.**

   o Taking regular breaks, including short walks, mental
     pauses, and vacations where you disconnect from
     work, can significantly improve leadership perfor-
     mance. Research shows that taking frequent breaks

helps manage stress, increases creativity, improves focus, and boosts overall well-being, all of which are essential for leaders.[14] Leaders who prioritize breaks tend to be more productive, make better decisions, and foster healthier work environments. This practice also reduces burnout by helping you recharge, leading to better clarity of thought, increased creativity, and improved long-term resilience.

By integrating these practices, you can develop a habit of reflection that enhances self-awareness, decision-making, and overall leadership effectiveness.

Leadership is a demanding role that requires intentionality and space in your schedule to perform at your best. It's easy for busy leaders to justify the lack of time for reflection, planning, and thoughtful decision-making, but exceptional leaders understand that dedicating time to these areas is crucial for success. By intentionally carving out time for reflection and strategic thinking, you gain clarity, make better decisions, and foster long-term success for yourself and your team. Time for these practices is not a luxury; it's an essential investment in your leadership effectiveness. Reflection is an important practice that enhances your leadership effectiveness and impact.

8

SELF-AWARENESS

He who knows others is wise;
he who knows himself is enlightened.

—Lao Tzu

I once reported to a brilliant executive: sharp, strategic, and deeply knowledgeable about our industry. Working with him pushed me to elevate my thinking, enhancing my strategic thinking and planning skills. However, he had a shadow side. While he encouraged others to voice ideas and take ownership of their departments, his actions often didn't align with his words.

I recall an executive meeting where a colleague challenged an idea, prompting the executive to become so angry that he stood up, grabbed his planner, and left the meeting. He didn't speak to the entire team for three days. I'm sure you can imagine the type of environment a leader can create when they react so negatively. We all felt like we were walking on eggshells, and quickly learned to pick our battles and rarely challenge the boss. This type of behavior creates an even bigger problem long-term: artificial harmony.

Artificial harmony occurs when team members go along with decisions without voicing concerns or offering differing perspectives—not because they agree, but because they want to avoid disrupting the status quo. Most often, this is a form of self-protection. If I know my boss might react negatively or lose his temper, I am more likely to stay silent to protect my own mental well-being and preserve the relationship.

After that meeting, I found myself constantly weighing whether it was worth speaking up. I began to ask: Do I want to have a productive day, or a stressful one? Challenging my boss meant risking conflict and tension; staying quiet meant I could avoid the emotional fallout. Over time, silence became the safer choice. And I wasn't alone.

Most employees are making that same calculation every day, often without realizing it. When leaders react negatively to pushback, they create an environment where employees choose self-preservation over contribution, and that ultimately erodes trust, engagement, and team effectiveness.

The long-term effects of artificial harmony are destructive to individuals, teams, and organizational cultures. When most or all of your employees don't feel comfortable speaking up, trust, cohesion, and collaboration are eroded.

Amy Edmondson, professor at Harvard University, coined the phrase "team psychological safety."[15] Psychological safety is a "shared belief held by members of a team that it's okay to take risks, to express their ideas and concerns, to speak up with questions, and to admit mistakes, all without fear of negative consequences." It's when team members feel permission to be honest.

Sometimes, artificial harmony shows up on teams where the individuals truly like each other and avoid confrontation because they don't want to harm the relationship. There are many causes of artificial harmony on teams, but the essence is that artificial harmony is not healthy in relationships, whether in a partnership or on a team. Constructive conflict is necessary for a healthy, high-functioning team.

Artificial harmony often persists not just because of team dynamics, but because leaders lack the self-awareness to recognize how their own behavior contributes to it.

I often see this in my work with teams: a technically skilled manager who struggles, not because they lack capability, but because they lack awareness of how their behavior affects others. These leaders often haven't taken the time to understand themselves or their impact, and some believe their approach is just who they are, expecting others to adapt. But that mindset limits growth. We learn from every leader we encounter—sometimes by modeling their strengths, and other times by recognizing what we don't want to replicate.

Self-awareness is an essential element of effective leadership. Thirty years ago, a transactional leadership style was often accepted, but in today's environment, emotional intelligence is critical for success. What have traditionally been called "soft skills" are, in fact, essential skills for leadership effectiveness today.

A self-aware leader is more likely to exercise sound judgment and make informed decisions. By understanding their values, biases, and motivations, they can align their choices with the organization's goals and principles. This awareness also helps minimize the risk of impulsive or emotionally driven decisions.

KEY ELEMENTS OF SELF-AWARENESS IN LEADERSHIP

- **Emotional Intelligence**: Recognize and regulate your own emotions while understanding how they impact your behavior and relationships.

- **Understanding Strengths and Weaknesses**: Leverage your strengths effectively and acknowledge areas for growth to enhance your leadership.

- **Behavioral Impact**: Be aware of how your words, actions, and decisions affect your team's morale, trust, and performance.

- **Personal Values and Beliefs**: Clarify your core values and ensure your leadership approach aligns with both your principles and your organization's culture.

- **Triggers and Stress Responses**: Identify what situations trigger stress or frustration and develop strategies to manage your reactions constructively.

- **Ability to Manage Stress Appropriately**: Maintain composure under pressure and avoid projecting stress onto your team.

> • **Openness to Feedback**: Actively seek out and receive feedback to gain insight into how others experience your leadership and identify opportunities to grow.

LEADERSHIP ASSESSMENTS FOR BUILDING AWARENESS

Leadership assessments are an effective way to deepen your understanding of your own leadership style and preferences and to build your self-awareness. While acknowledging that no assessment is flawless—each possesses its strengths and limitations—they can provide valuable insights for fostering self-awareness and initiating meaningful team discussions. It's important to note that leadership assessments are not intended for diagnostic purposes; rather, they are best used to cultivate awareness and encourage dialogue within teams. It's crucial to recognize that no assessment can comprehensively capture the entirety of an individual, and not every aspect in an assessment report will perfectly align with each person's unique qualities. However, assessments can provide a useful framework for exploring what resonates, what doesn't, and for sparking meaningful dialogue on how to work better together.

Using leadership assessments is an excellent way to learn more about your own style, preferences, and behaviors, as well as their impact on others. They are also a valuable tool for understanding others' needs, preferences, behaviors, and style. The best leaders use this information to adjust their approach with others. This is what emotional intelligence is all about—having the wisdom to understand that not everyone is like you, and to take time to pause, reflect, and respond with intention rather than reacting with emotion.

Below are the individual assessments I most commonly use with leaders and teams.

1. **CliftonStrengths Assessment**: The CliftonStrengths assessment, developed by Gallup, focuses on identifying and leveraging individuals' strengths. It categorizes 34 signature themes to provide insights into one's unique combination of talents,

empowering individuals to maximize their potential in various aspects of life, including leadership and personal growth.

2. **Myers-Briggs Type Indicator® (MBTI®):** The Myers-Briggs Type Indicator is a widely used personality assessment that categorizes individuals into 16 personality types based on preferences related to four dichotomies. It offers insights into how people perceive the world, make decisions, and interact with others, contributing to a better understanding and communication in both personal and professional settings.

3. **Everything DiSC® Management:** DiSC is a behavior assessment tool published by Wiley that classifies individuals into four primary personality styles: Dominance, Influence, Steadiness, and Conscientiousness. This assessment helps individuals comprehend their communication preferences, management style, motivators, stressors, and how they interact with others. I like how this assessment offers multiple report types that focus specifically on an area, such as Workplace, Productive Conflict, Agile EQ, and Work of Leaders.

4. **EQi 2.0 (Emotional Intelligence):** The EQi 2.0 is an emotional intelligence assessment that measures an individual's emotional and social skills. It evaluates areas such as self-perception, interpersonal relationships, stress management, and decision-making. This assessment is valuable for personal development, enhancing leadership capabilities, and fostering effective collaboration within teams.

Used constructively, assessments can be a valuable tool individually, as well as on teams. As a leader, knowing the strengths and weaknesses of your team members helps you to manage them more effectively.

ANY STRENGTH OVERUSED CAN BECOME A LIABILITY

Understanding your strengths is a great starting point, but even our greatest talents, when overused or unchecked, can become obstacles rather than assets. This concept applies across many leadership and personality assessments, but for the purpose of this example, I'm using the CliftonStrengths assessment. It identifies your unique talents—your natural patterns of thinking, feeling, and behaving—and categorizes them into themes.[16] Based on Gallup's research on performance excellence, they have found that employees who understand and productively apply their strengths at work are more engaged, productive, and report a higher quality of life. This assessment helps you understand yourself better and what energizes you. It also helps you see what you aren't naturally good at and how to manage those areas.

> ANY STRENGTH OVERUSED CAN BECOME A LIABILITY.

While identifying and applying your strengths is incredibly valuable, it's equally important to recognize that those same strengths, when overused or unbalanced, can become blind spots that hinder your effectiveness. Any strength overused can become a liability.

My top theme from CliftonStrengths is Achiever—"people exceptionally talented in Achiever work hard and possess a great deal of stamina. They take immense satisfaction in being busy and productive."[17] This strength has helped me greatly in my professional and personal life. I have an excellent work ethic, work through issues, commit to and follow through on goals, and am highly productive in my work. Channeled productively, this strength has immense value in my life. I've learned that while these strengths serve me well, there are times when overusing them can turn them into liabilities. Building self-awareness means not just understanding what I do well, but also recognizing when a strength crosses the line from helpful to counterproductive.

For me, over-relying on my Achiever theme once translated into long hours, being overly focused on goals, and placing too much emphasis on productivity. Earlier in my career, that intensity sometimes hindered my leadership: I pushed myself past healthy limits and created unnecessary pressure for myself and others. Over time, I realized that when my drive isn't balanced, it can become a liability, so I started paying closer attention to the moments when my Achiever tendencies needed to be dialed back. I had noticed this pattern in my work life before, but over time, I began to see it showing up at home as well—creating unnecessary stress for me and my family.

One pattern still shows up the night before a business trip. My stress rises, and I slip into hyper-focused "get it done" mode, often at the expense of empathy. I find myself rushing my kids through bedtime and reacting impatiently. Being aware of this, I've learned to pause, shift gears, and focus on being present. Without that self-awareness, overusing this strength could strain the relationships I value most and erode the close relationship I want to cultivate with my kids.

By enhancing our self-awareness and understanding the potential drawbacks of our strengths, we can create healthier personal and professional connections, ensuring that our strengths truly serve us and those around us. It also enables us to leverage the diverse and complementary strengths of our colleagues, creating enhanced performance and better outcomes.

I mentioned previously that conflict avoidance is a common challenge that negatively impacts leadership. While the ability to foster harmony is a valuable strength when applied constructively, leaders who prioritize harmony may inadvertently overuse it by avoiding difficult conversations. This tendency might manifest in avoiding addressing issues with a negative or underperforming employee, which can detrimentally affect the team and overall workplace culture. Recognizing this potential pitfall allows a leader to proactively manage this quality, ensuring it remains an asset rather than a liability.

Self-awareness enhances your ability to understand yourself, relate to others, and navigate complex leadership challenges. It contributes to creating a positive and productive work environment, fostering collaboration, and ultimately driving organizational success.

Exceptional leaders understand that diverse personalities, generations, backgrounds, and experiences shape how individuals see the world. By being intentional in how you engage with others and adapting your approach to connect effectively, you expand your leadership influence and make a greater impact.

STRATEGIES FOR CULTIVATING SELF-AWARENESS

Engaging in leadership assessments is one way to consistently build your self-awareness and advance your leadership development.

Here are four more ways to increase self-awareness.

1. **Solicit Feedback from Those Around You.**

   Whether it's a formal 360-degree feedback tool or simply asking for regular feedback from your employees, peers, and manager, be curious enough to ask and open enough to listen to what people have to say.

   Part of developing, growing, and building confidence is getting feedback from those around you. Yet, most managers are terrible at providing feedback, especially meaningful feedback. In fact, research shows that women tend to receive very vague feedback throughout their careers, while men generally receive more tangible, results-focused feedback.[18] So, while feedback is often biased, there are ways you can encourage more specific, meaningful feedback.

   Ask Focused, Refined Questions.

   Refining your questions can make a big difference in the quality of feedback you receive. Broad questions like "Can you give me feedback?" or "How am I doing?" can be overwhelming for the person you are asking. It forces them to recall all their experiences with you, which can lead to vague answers like "you're doing a great job," which isn't very helpful.

   Instead, try asking more specific, focused questions that are easier for others to process and answer:

   - What is one of my strengths, and one area for improvement?
   - What's one thing I'm doing well that I should keep doing?
   - What's one area I should work on to improve?

- What's one skill or focus area I should develop in the next three months?
- What are two things I can do to support you better?
- What is something I should start doing/stop doing/continue doing?
- What is working well? What is not working well? What can I do to support you better? (These are also great questions to use for improving team dynamics. You can reframe them to: What is working well on the team? What is not working well on the team?)

I don't recommend asking all of these questions at once—pick one or two based on your feedback goals. Another great way to gain constructive feedback is to ask colleagues. Some possible questions:

- What is one thing I can do to support you better?
- What is one thing that can continue to strengthen our relationship?

If you are working on developing in a specific area, asking a colleague for support and feedback can be a great way to gain constructive feedback and build your confidence. For example, if you want to get better at speaking up in meetings in a concise manner, ask a colleague to observe you in meetings over the next three weeks and take notes on what you do well and what you can improve upon. A trusted colleague can be a great support in building skills. Before a tough conversation, talk it through with a trusted colleague and role-play how you will handle the issue.

2. **Master Your Emotional Triggers.**

    Understanding and evaluating your negative emotional triggers is a key aspect of building self-awareness and improving your leadership. When you're aware of what provokes strong emotional reactions, you can better manage your responses, ensuring that decisions and actions are grounded in rational thought rather than impulse. This self-regulation not only helps you stay calm under pressure but also sets a positive example for others.

A great practice is to actively notice over the next two weeks situations, events, or interactions that create a negative emotional reaction in you. Take some time to reflect on why this particular trigger is coming up for you. By addressing and understanding these triggers, you can become more intentional with how you manage them. You will increase your emotional intelligence, ultimately leading to stronger, more effective leadership.

3. **Continuous Growth.**

In an ever-evolving world, effective leadership demands ongoing personal development. Reading leadership and business books, listening to insightful podcasts, and actively pursuing training and development initiatives will continually enhance your leadership skills.

4. **Engage with a Coach or Mentor.**

Whether it's someone you respect in your organization or industry, or an objective leadership coach, engaging with a mentor or coach can provide ongoing support and development as you navigate leadership and life challenges.

Fostering curiosity about your own thoughts, perceptions, and behaviors is the key to enhancing self-knowledge, ensuring continuous learning, adaptation, and growth in your leadership journey. In the upcoming chapter, we will delve into the significance of energy as a critical leadership skill—because the energy you bring to your work, your team, and your interactions directly shapes your influence and impact.

9

THE ENERGY EDGE—FUELING LEADERSHIP EXCELLENCE

Success doesn't just come from hustle—it comes from managing your energy, not just your time.

—Jim Loehr & Tony Schwartz

Our culture glorifies busyness, treating packed schedules and long hours as a badge of honor and a requirement for success. The prevailing belief is that working harder and longer is the only way to get ahead. High-profile entrepreneurs like Elon Musk, who famously works 120-hour weeks, and Grant Cardone, who puts in 95-hour weeks, reinforce the idea that success requires relentless work, outworking the competition at all costs. But this old-school mindset of working ourselves to exhaustion is not a sustainable or effective path to success.

As I researched this chapter, I noticed a common pattern: many of the loudest voices advocating extreme work hours were men. Their advice often boiled down to one mindset: work more, sleep less, and hustle harder. But just as employee expectations have evolved, so must leadership. With a greater recognition of the importance of well-being, balance, and sustainable productivity, we need a new model—one that allows us to perform at our best without burning out.

I'm not suggesting that there aren't times when working long hours is necessary, especially for entrepreneurs in high-growth startups or industries with demanding seasons. However, for most leaders, the constant grind doesn't make us better; it drains us and reduces productivity. Overworking doesn't just deplete energy; it diminishes decision-making, stifles creativity, and leads to disengagement.

Fortunately, not all successful leaders buy into the "hustle at all costs" mentality. Many high achievers understand that managing energy and focus, not time, is the key to peak performance. Meghan Hyatt, CEO of Full Focus, intentionally works six-hour days so she can be home to greet her children after school.[19] Annie Tevelin, CEO of beauty brand Skinowl, instituted a four-day workweek for her company.[20] Jason Fried, CEO of Basecamp, sticks to a strict 40-hour workweek.[21] Even entire companies, like Swedish tech firm Brath, have adopted six-hour workdays, reporting higher productivity and increased employee engagement.[22] These leaders prove that long hours don't equal better results—focused, intentional work does.

Every business is different, and I'm not suggesting that managers can always limit themselves to a strict 40-hour workweek. However, in my experience, most leaders who find themselves working unsustainable hours lack the necessary structures and focus skills to create exceptional results. They often operate under the amateur model—reacting to demands and constantly playing catch-up—rather than the professional model of proactively managing their energy, focus, and priorities to achieve more in less time.

I've personally learned to compartmentalize my time to get better results. At work, I'm hyper-focused and intentional with my schedule. At home, I strive to be fully present with my family. Of course, there are moments of overwhelm, and occasionally, extra hours are required. But overall, I've found that I am far more productive, focused, and effective within a structured 40-hour workweek than I would be if I blurred the lines between work and personal time. Boundaries aren't limitations; they are tools that support professionals to work at their best.

THE ROLE OF REST IN HIGH PERFORMANCE

What we do outside of work directly impacts how we perform at work. Sleep, exercise, and mental recovery aren't indulgences; they're essential for sustained success. We need to stop treating sleep as negotiable and stop perpetuating the myth that successful people don't have time to rest. In reality, many of the world's most successful leaders prioritize sleep. Jeff Bezos, Arianna Huffington, Barack Obama, and Bill Gates all emphasize the importance of rest. Arianna Huffington wrote *The Sleep Revolution* to raise awareness of how sleep fuels performance.[23]

Energy management is one of the most overlooked yet powerful factors in leadership. It affects how we show up, how we perform, and how we influence those around us. Energy fuels effective leadership, shaping your mindset, decisions, and interactions. Just as a machine needs the right fuel to function optimally, leaders must manage their energy to stay focused, resilient, and engaged.

THE LEADERSHIP ENERGY FRAMEWORK

There are several elements of energy that we will explore in this chapter, each playing a vital role in how effectively you lead. Consider what needs to happen for you to operate at your best. For me, a great night's sleep is crucial—losing even one hour affects my stamina, performance, and memory. But energy isn't just about how we feel; it's also about what we project. What energy do you convey to others? Are you showing up engaged, focused, and present, or are you drained, distracted, and reactive?

Leadership requires more than just pushing through exhaustion—it demands intentional energy management. That means optimizing how you recharge, eliminating energy drains, and structuring your day for peak performance. When you take control of your energy, you set the foundation for better decisions, stronger relationships, and a greater impact in your leadership.

I created the Leadership Energy Framework to highlight the essential aspects of energy and its crucial impact on leadership. This framework helps leaders optimize energy across three key areas.

- **core energy** (physical and mental well-being)
- **performance energy** (focus and productivity)
- **relational energy** (the impact you have on others)

Performance

Relational

Core

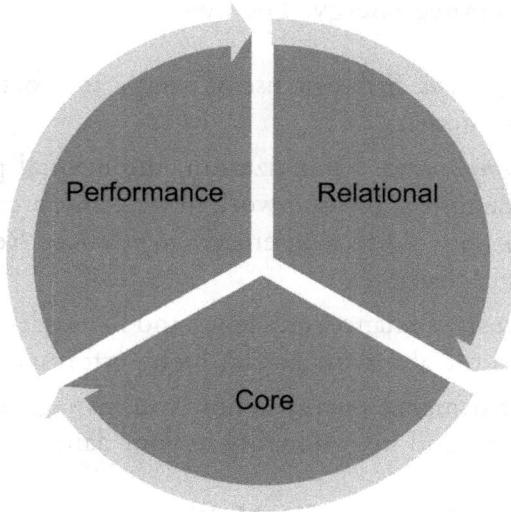

Each plays a vital role in leadership effectiveness, ensuring resilience, peak performance, and meaningful connections. Mastering energy isn't about pushing through exhaustion; it's about intentionally sustaining and directing it to create meaningful impact. The way you manage your energy directly impacts your personal productivity and amplifies your leadership influence.

1. **Core Energy: The Foundation**

   o *Key Focus*: Physical and mental energy. Personal renewal and resilience.
   o *Components*: Sleep quality, regular rest, healthy habits, physical activity, healthy boundaries, and recharge.
   o *Impact*: Boosts cognitive clarity, emotional regulation, and overall stamina for leadership demands. Enhances performance at work and home.
   o Core energy is the foundation—your physical well-being, mindset, and overall capacity to lead with resilience.

2. Performance Energy: The Engine

- *Key Focus*: Strategic use of energy and focus for optimal productivity.
- *Components*: Prioritization, intentional planning and scheduling, focused work blocks, and breaks to prevent burnout. Directing energy to the Key Result Areas of your position.
- *Impact*: Enhances efficiency and focus, decision-making, and the ability to sustain high performance over time.
- Performance energy is how you manage focus, productivity, and intentionality in your daily work.

3. Relational Energy: The Multiplier

- *Key Focus*: How the energy you generate influences and impacts others.
- *Components*: Positive interactions, emotional contagion, presence in conversations, and cultivating a motivating environment.
- *Impact*: Strengthens team engagement, collaboration, and organizational culture.
- Relational energy is the impact you have on others—the emotional tone, presence, and engagement you bring to every interaction.

Each dimension reinforces the others, creating a dynamic cycle where physical well-being enhances focus at work, effective workplace habits sustain energy for high-impact results, and strong relationships empower the team to perform at its best.

Great leadership isn't just about what you do; it's about the energy you cultivate and project. Each element plays a critical role in your effectiveness, ensuring that you remain resilient in the face of challenges, perform at your best, and foster positive, energizing relationships with your team. In this chapter, we'll explore how mastering these three dimensions can elevate your leadership and create a lasting, positive impact.

As leaders, the energy we bring to our roles directly influences our ability to lead, make decisions, and inspire our teams. Most leaders don't fully recognize the connection between personal well-being and leadership effectiveness. Ensuring proper rest, recovery, and reflection is essential for managing energy and leading with sustained focus and purpose.

The Energy Leadership Framework doesn't just enhance your leadership abilities; it also elevates your personal life, bringing greater balance and fulfillment to every aspect of your day. By optimizing your energy across core, performance, and relational areas, you gain stamina and resilience to manage both professional and personal demands. When you're intentional about how you use your energy, you can show up as a more present and engaged partner, parent, or friend, creating deeper connections and fostering positive relationships outside of work.

This holistic approach ensures that your leadership extends beyond the office, allowing you to lead with purpose, reduce stress, and create harmony between your career and personal life, ultimately leading to greater satisfaction and well-being.

Let's explore these three aspects of energy and how you can use them to enhance leadership and personal success.

1. CORE ENERGY: THE FOUNDATION

Have you ever had a night when you barely slept, then noticed the next day how everything at work felt harder? Your focus drifts, small problems feel bigger, and your patience wears thin. Even one night of poor sleep can make a clear difference in how you think, communicate, and lead—and if it happens often, the impact on your performance and relationships can be significant. For leaders, physical energy isn't optional; it's the base layer that supports clear judgment, steady presence, and the ability to positively influence others.

Leaders who prioritize their physical energy build the foundation for resilience, renewal, and sustained success. Key aspects of physical energy include quality sleep, regular movement, healthy habits, and intentional rest. Managing energy—both at work and outside of it—is essential for peak performance. Your personal energy bank encompasses physical, emotional, and mental reserves, all of which are necessary to influence others and achieve meaningful results.

Yet, many leaders are sleep-deprived, overworked, and trapped in a cycle where long hours and busyness are mistaken for productivity. A study by the Center for Creative Leadership found that 42 percent of leaders get less than the recommended six hours of sleep a night.[24] The impact of poor sleep includes poor judgment, diminished creativity, and a lack of self-control. In that study, researchers found that managers who lacked sleep were more irritable, impatient, and hostile toward their employees. Not only does a lack of sleep impact a leader's decisions and personal productivity, but it also has a negative impact on employee engagement, productivity, and decision-making.

BECOMING YOUR BEST EXERCISE

What does it take for you to operate at your best? Identifying what isn't working is just as important as recognizing what fuels you. No one is perfect, and even with the best intentions, we sometimes fall into habits that drain our energy. The key is to recognize what you need to operate at your best so you can be intentional about your core energy.

I thrive on structure and routine, but when my schedule gets disrupted, I sometimes slip into patterns that don't serve me. I recall one spring break when my kids were home while my husband, Rino, and I were working. Instead of their usual school schedule, we juggled drop-offs at camp in the morning and childcare with my mother-in-law in the afternoon. By the end of each day, we were drained from managing work and family logistics. That first night, I told my husband I was too tired to read and suggested we watch the TV show *Billions* instead. One episode turned into seven straight nights of binge-watching, pushing our bedtime later than usual. A little mindless TV seemed harmless—until it wasn't.

That week, I felt the consequences of not getting enough sleep: reduced focus, lower productivity, and mounting fatigue. Even answering a simple email felt hard, and by the end of the week, my patience with my kids was wearing thin. Whenever I deviate from the habits that help me feel and perform at my best, I almost always regret it.

It took just a couple of nights of good sleep to reset, and the difference in my energy and focus was immediate. Sleep is one of the most underrated success habits, and when pressed for time, I often prioritize it over other practices like meditation or yoga. The quality of my sleep directly impacts my ability to lead, think clearly, and show up fully.

The habits we cultivate—both good and bad—shape how we lead every day.

THREE REFLECTION QUESTIONS

- What habits or routines help you feel and perform at your best, and where do you tend to fall off track?
- How do disruptions in your schedule impact your energy, focus, and leadership presence? What strategies can you use to recover more quickly?
- Which of the four key elements—sleep, movement, mindset, or boundaries—needs the most attention in your life right now, and what is one change you can make to improve it?

I've found that managing my energy in three-day cycles works well for me. For example, if I have a big presentation on a Tuesday, the choices I make in the days leading up to it—how I sleep, eat, and recharge—directly impact my energy and performance. Likewise, if I'm out late on a Saturday night, it takes about three days to fully rebalance my energy.

Being aware of these patterns helps me stay intentional about how I prepare for key moments. Recognizing personal needs—whether it's limiting screen time, prioritizing exercise, or setting boundaries—ensures sustained energy and effectiveness both at work and at home.

Getting adequate sleep and managing stress are important elements of successful leadership. Inspiring and engaging others requires energy and influence. For you to bring out the best in others, you have to be at your best.

To lead effectively, leaders must take ownership of their energy. High-quality sleep sharpens cognitive clarity and emotional regulation, enabling better decision-making and composure under stress. Regular movement, healthy eating habits, and intentional breaks sustain stamina and focus, while healthy boundaries—such as true disconnection—prevent burnout. By prioritizing these foundational elements, you enhance both your professional performance and personal well-being, creating the capacity to show up as your best self every day.

2. PERFORMANCE ENERGY: THE ENGINE

Performance energy is the driving force behind a leader's ability to execute, make decisions, and sustain productivity over time. It's not just about working hard; it's about working with intention. Leaders who manage their performance energy effectively don't waste time reacting to distractions or getting lost in low-impact tasks. Instead, they channel their energy toward the most important aspects of their role, ensuring their time and effort align with their Key Result Areas.

At the heart of performance energy is strategic focus. This means prioritizing what truly moves the needle, planning your work intentionally, and structuring your day to optimize both energy and efficiency. Effective leaders use focused work blocks to tackle high-value tasks without interruptions, schedule breaks to recharge and maintain mental clarity, and avoid the common trap of filling their day with busyness rather than meaningful progress. When leaders fail to manage their energy wisely, they risk burnout, decision fatigue, and diminished effectiveness.

The impact of performance energy extends beyond daily productivity: it shapes a leader's long-term success. When energy is directed intentionally, leaders make better, more thoughtful decisions, maintain greater resilience under pressure, and cultivate a more sustainable work rhythm. By mastering prioritization, intentional planning, and energy management, leaders not only enhance their own performance but also create an environment where their teams can thrive.

As we explored earlier, amateurs allow their energy to be dictated by distractions, reacting to whatever demands their attention in the moment. Professionals, however, take ownership of their energy, directing it with intention toward what truly matters. They prioritize, plan, and protect their focus, knowing that high performance isn't about being constantly busy; it's about being consistently effective. By managing performance energy like a pro, leaders set themselves up for sustained success and greater impact.

3. Relational Energy: The Multiplier

Energy isn't just personal; it's contagious. The way you show up, the energy you bring into a room, and your presence in conversations all influence those around you. This is what makes relational energy so powerful. Whether through positive interactions, emotional contagion, or simply being present, leaders set the tone for their teams and organizations. Strong relational energy fosters engagement, collaboration, and a culture where people feel valued and motivated. But just as positive energy can uplift a team, negative energy can just as easily drain it.

A few years ago, I switched to a new chiropractor. When I walked into the office for my first appointment, the receptionist barely looked up as she unenthusiastically muttered, "Yes?" Her lack of warmth had an immediate impact: I felt my energy drop. Instead of feeling welcomed, I felt like an inconvenience. That one interaction shaped my entire experience in the office, and I found myself less enthusiastic about returning. We've all encountered service professionals who seem disconnected from their role, and it's a reminder of how much first impressions and energy matter.

Organizations train customer-facing employees to be friendly and engaging, yet far too often, they place people in these roles who don't enjoy interacting with others. The same is true in leadership—whether we realize it or not, the energy we bring each day leaves a lasting impression on our teams.

As a leader, you are constantly being observed. Your demeanor, your energy, and your presence influence your employees, colleagues, and even *your* manager. Whether consciously or subconsciously, people pick up on your emotional state. If you consistently appear stressed, overwhelmed, or disengaged, that energy transfers to those around you. On the other hand, when you show up with presence, focus, and positive energy, you create an environment where others feel empowered to do their best work.

Every morning, as you step into the office or join a Zoom call, ask yourself: What tone am I setting? Do I greet my employees with warmth and enthusiasm, or do I appear distracted and rushed? During meetings, am I fully present and engaged, or am I checking my phone and half-listening? Leadership is about more than just the words you say; it's about the energy you bring into every interaction.

This doesn't mean leaders must always be upbeat or suppress their emotions. It's about awareness and intentionality. The energy you bring into a room influences the people around you, whether you intend it to or not. Employees look to their leaders for cues on how to behave, and they often mirror the energy they receive from them. Leadership is not just about setting expectations; it's about modeling them. When you take ownership of your relational energy, you create an environment where engagement, collaboration, and high performance can thrive.

> THE ENERGY YOU BRING INTO A ROOM INFLUENCES THE PEOPLE AROUND YOU, WHETHER YOU INTEND IT TO OR NOT.

Research from Northwestern University's Kellogg School of Management highlights just how contagious energy and performance can be. The study found that employees who sat within 25 feet of a high-performing colleague experienced a 15 percent boost in their own performance, while those near a low performer saw a 30 percent decline.[25] This reinforces a crucial leadership lesson: energy is infectious. The way leaders (and employees) show up every day directly influences their colleagues. When leaders bring focus, enthusiasm, and a strong work ethic, they elevate those around them. But when they exhibit stress, disengagement, or negativity, that energy spreads just as quickly, dragging down performance. As managers, we must be intentional about the energy we project, knowing that it has a ripple effect on our teams and organizational culture.

It's equally important for managers to recognize when an employee's energy is consistently draining the team. An individual who regularly complains, resists cooperation, or projects negativity doesn't just impact their own work—they affect the mindset, motivation, and performance of those around them. Part of a manager's responsibility is to address these patterns directly, providing support or setting clear expectations to protect the overall health of the team environment.

Several years ago, I hired a parenting coach because I was struggling with how to handle certain interactions with my kids. The very tools I was known for and practiced consistently in my professional life—pausing before reacting, asking thoughtful questions, and leading with intention—were surprisingly difficult to implement at home. I often found myself overwhelmed and reactive, unsure how to handle emotionally charged situations with my children, even though I coached others through similar challenges in the workplace.

I wanted to be more patient, more intentional, and more confident—but I didn't know how to get there on my own.

One of the most eye-opening realizations was just how much my energy influenced the tone in our home, often more than my words or intentions. Instead of trying to fix *them*, I needed to focus on myself and how I was showing up in the interaction. For years, when my kids walked in after school, my first instinct was to zero in on what wasn't right—snapping at them to pick up their coats or put their shoes away. That initial negativity often set the tone for the entire evening, leading to unnecessary power struggles at bedtime. But when I became more intentional about how I greeted them, focusing on connection instead of correction, everything began to shift. People, especially children, tend to mirror the energy we project to them. As I changed my approach, my kids (usually) responded in kind. It was a simple but powerful reminder: the energy we bring into any moment shapes what happens next.

Energy is one of the most valuable assets a leader has, yet too many sacrifice it in the name of busyness. To lead effectively, we must shift our mindset, prioritizing energy management as a strategic advantage rather than an afterthought. Sleep should be viewed as a success habit, not a luxury. When leaders prioritize their own rest and set the example by encouraging healthy boundaries in the workplace, it creates a ripple effect. Sustainable leadership isn't about working the longest hours; it's about showing up with clarity, focus, and the energy to lead with impact. When we take ownership of our energy, we not only elevate our own performance, but we create a culture where everyone benefits.

In the coming chapters, we'll shift our focus to the essential skills needed to build and sustain a thriving team. The ability to create clarity, cultivate a strong culture, and facilitate results requires both internal and external leadership mastery. Reflection, self-awareness, and energy management lay the foundation for how we show up, think critically, and engage with others. Without the capacity to manage our own energy, it becomes far more difficult to lead effectively. By strengthening these internal elements, we equip ourselves to lead with greater clarity, purpose, and impact, ensuring that both we and our teams can perform at our best.

PART 3

LEAD WITH CONFIDENCE, CLARITY, AND RESULTS

10

FROM CHAOS TO CLARITY: MASTERING YOUR FOCUS

*Only once you give yourself permission to stop trying to do it all,
to stop saying yes to everyone, can you make your highest
contribution toward the things that really matter.*

—Greg McKeown

In today's fast-paced world of endless information, constant interruptions, and competing demands, clarity isn't just helpful—it's essential for effective leadership. Yet, many leaders find themselves consumed by low-value tasks and distractions that pull them away from their most important responsibilities. One of the most damaging leadership saboteurs is a lack of clarity around where to focus. If you spend your days reacting rather than leading, you won't be able to guide your team to meaningful results.

> This section will explore how to create clarity in two important areas.
>
> - **Personal Clarity & Productivity:** Defining your priorities and managing your time effectively.
> - **Team Clarity & Productivity:** Ensuring your team has a clear understanding of their responsibilities, priorities, and expectations.

We'll begin with your personal productivity as a leader because, before you can guide a high-performing team, you must first master your own focus and priorities. Next, we'll dive into creating clarity for your team, ensuring they have the direction and structure needed to deliver exceptional results. Finally, I'll share strategies for leading clear, intentional, and impactful meetings so you can maximize time, achieve results, and avoid wasted effort.

The strategies I'm about to share aren't revolutionary—they're timeless. In fact, it's often the simplest strategies and structures that enable us to perform at our best. Yet, many people undervalue these foundational principles, dismissing them as too basic to make a real impact.

Success isn't just about knowledge—it's about consistently applying the right habits and actions that support results.

Legendary basketball coach John Wooden understood this well. No matter how many championships his team won, he always started each season the same way: by teaching his players how to properly put on their socks and tie their shoes. He knew that a single blister or sprained ankle could sideline a player and cost the team a game. The fundamentals mattered, and Wooden never wavered in reinforcing them.

The same is true for leadership. Productivity tools and focus strategies may seem basic, but they are the foundation of success. Don't underestimate the power of simple, intentional practices that build a strong leadership foundation. How you choose to spend your time isn't just a daily decision; it's a strategic one that determines your impact and effectiveness as a leader.

Strategies for Personal Clarity and Productivity

Have you ever left work at the end of a long day, and you know you were busy—you spent the day doing a lot of things—but you couldn't really pinpoint what you accomplished? You spent all day dealing with low-level tasks, interruptions, emails, and meetings, but you didn't have time to get to the *real* work? This is how most leaders

> PRODUCTIVITY IS THE FOUNDATION OF EXCEPTIONAL LEADERSHIP.

are operating on a daily basis. They are operating in *activity* mode, not *accomplishment* mode. Most managers spend their days fighting interruptions and distractions, sitting in unproductive meetings, and reacting to the problems and issues that constantly come their way.

Productivity is the foundation of exceptional leadership. All successful leaders leverage their time and resources effectively. If you can't manage your priorities, you will never have enough time to focus on other important areas for leadership success, like coaching, providing feedback, developing your team, and creating a strategy. To work at peak productivity, you need to be able to control your attention, so you can create great visions, implement great strategies, and execute.

Being a leader today is more complex than it has ever been. In our modern society, we are bombarded with information every day. Emails, text messages, marketing messages, blogs, social media, and the Internet all contribute to information overload. More information has its benefits, but it can also be overwhelming, leaving us paralyzed from taking action. All of our electronic devices can be great tools, yet for most people, they are a source of great distraction.

Advancements in technology have created a hyper-addiction to constant connectivity, making it increasingly difficult for leaders to focus on what truly matters. Continuous Partial Attention (CPA), a term coined by Linda Stone, describes the tendency to be in a constant state of alertness, scanning the world but never fully engaging.[26] While this behavior may feel productive, it actually fragments focus, weakens decision-making, and pulls leaders away from key results that drive success.

Ineffective leadership often stems from this scattered attention, as frequent interruptions, excessive phone use, and multitasking dilute strategic thinking and meaningful work. Over time, the physiological effects of CPA—elevated cortisol and adrenaline—create a cycle of stress and distraction that fuels the addiction to checking in. To counteract this, leaders must master the essential skill of single-tasking: dedicating their full attention to one priority at a time. The ability to cut through noise, eliminate unnecessary distractions, and deeply focus on high-impact initiatives is not just a productivity strategy; it's a leadership imperative.

Psychologists from Columbia and Stanford Universities conducted a study on how too many options can affect decision-making.[27] At an upscale food market, they set up a tasting table offering 24 varieties of jam. On another day, the same table featured just six varieties. While the larger display attracted more attention, shoppers who encountered only six options were ten times more likely to make a purchase. The researchers found that too many choices can overwhelm people, making them less likely to decide at all, a phenomenon known as *choice paralysis*.

This same concept of choice paralysis shows up in leadership as well, only instead of jam, it's our time, attention, and energy that are spread too thin. We have so many things we can work on that we become overwhelmed and don't know where to start. The excessive choices and demands of where to put our attention leave us feeling paralyzed, so we muddle through our day, working on trivial tasks that fill up the time. When we aren't intentional with our focus and energy, we will never find time for non-urgent yet important areas of leadership, like feedback, coaching, and strategizing. We keep hoping that one day soon, we will catch up and will finally have time for these other areas of leadership we just don't have time for.

One of the most important realizations I had to come to as a manager was that I was never going to feel fully "caught up." I thought that if I could speed up my production and work longer hours, I would finally be in a place where I could fit in these other non-urgent elements. But we will never catch up. Our job is to be on top of the most important areas that contribute to our key results.

Choose to Be Purposeful

The first thing you must do is realize that *you* have the biggest impact on how your day goes.

Yes, there will be unexpected interruptions, occasional emergencies, and things that come up. The world will always be chaotic, challenging, busy, and overwhelming. The ability to step back, cut through the clutter, and focus is what separates exceptional leaders from mediocre ones. It doesn't matter how talented you are. Success isn't possible if you're too consumed by the day-to-day to use your strengths and contribute at your highest level.

William James famously stated, "The essence of genius is knowing what to overlook," emphasizing that true wisdom lies in selective focus.[28] In leadership, effectiveness follows the same principle: **you become effective by being selective,** prioritizing what truly matters, and eliminating distractions that dilute impact.

You must choose to be purposeful each day.

As I shared in an earlier chapter, the energy we bring into a space has a powerful influence on the interactions that follow. One practice that helps me stay intentional about this is setting clear intentions throughout my day. As I transition into a new phase—whether it's a meeting, a conversation, or focused work, I pause and ask myself how I want to show up.

For example, before logging on to a meeting with a team member, I take a moment to set an intention to be fully present and focused, and I eliminate any distractions. This simple habit has become especially valuable in a fast-paced day filled with back-to-back meetings. Managers often move from one thing to the next without margin, which leads to reactive leadership. Taking a Purposeful Pause and setting an intention helps you reset your energy and mindset so you can bring your best to the moment ahead.

THE POWER OF FOCUS

Focus is what turns leadership potential into real results. You can have insight, vision, and emotional intelligence, but without the ability to consistently direct your attention to what matters most, your impact will remain limited. What sets high-performing leaders apart is their ability to filter distractions, stay grounded in their priorities, and invest their energy where it creates the greatest value.

Increasing efficiency comes down to two key factors.

1. **Clarity:** Knowing exactly what you need to accomplish. Many leaders struggle simply because they're unclear on their priorities.

2. **Focus:** The discipline to concentrate on high-value tasks and see them through to completion.

Leaders who move faster and achieve more have clarity on what truly matters and where to direct their energy. Without clear priorities, leadership becomes reactive, driven by tasks rather than results. A lack of clarity around key areas of focus often leads people to spend time on low-value, unimportant tasks.

The first step to increasing clarity, sharpening focus, and creating results is to define your **Key Result Areas (KRAs)**—the essential priorities that will make the greatest impact.

DEFINE YOUR KEY RESULT AREAS

One of the biggest productivity challenges for leaders is a lack of clarity on where to focus. With so many demands competing for attention, focus becomes a struggle.

The key to intentional productivity is defining your KRAs—the three to five core responsibilities that define your role and create real impact and results. KRAs are the essential tasks that only you can do. Without clear KRAs, leaders fall into a reactive cycle, letting meetings, distractions, and interruptions dictate their day.

I first learned this concept from Brian Tracy's book, *Eat That Frog*, a must-read for practical time management strategies.[29] Traditional job descriptions list tasks but lack clarity on results. By focusing on KRAs, leaders can prioritize high-value work, delegate distractions, and stay aligned with what truly makes the biggest impact.

Here are some questions to help guide you in developing your Key Result Areas.

- Why was my position created? What is the purpose of the position?
- What are the main results this position is intended to achieve?
- What is the difference between my job and the job of my staff members?
- What value does this position bring to the organization that other positions do not?
- What are the elements of my role that are my main responsibility and cannot be delegated or outsourced?

For example, when I was a human resources executive at a credit union, the Key Result Areas for my position were:

1. Position the organization as a top employer of choice by enhancing the employee experience and building a compelling employer brand.
2. Strengthen workforce performance and engagement through strategic development initiatives, leadership capability building, and culture alignment.
3. Build leadership capability across the organization by equipping managers with the skills, tools, and coaching to lead high-performing teams.
4. Align organizational structure, roles, and talent strategies to maximize individual strengths and organizational effectiveness.

Notice that the KRAs for an HR executive don't include directly overseeing benefits, payroll, compensation, or employee relations. While the executive may hold ultimate accountability, these operational functions are typically managed by their team. The HR manager might ensure these areas run smoothly day-to-day, but the executive's value lies in their ability to create the high-level strategy that guides the entire HR function. Their unique combination of experience, industry knowledge, leadership skills, and professional certifications equips them to craft forward-thinking strategies aligned with business goals. Only they have the perspective and expertise to design and influence the roadmap that facilitates long-term cultural success.

Each key result area can typically be broken down into specific projects or areas of focus.

Let's take the first key result area outlined above: **Position the organization as a top employer of choice by enhancing employee experience and building a compelling employer brand.**

This KRA can encompass several goals and projects. For example:

a) Design and implement a competitive, market-informed benefits package that supports employee well-being and retention.

b) Foster a culture of belonging, purpose, and recognition where employees feel valued and inspired to do their best work.

c) Equip people leaders with the training, coaching, and tools to create exceptional employee experiences and highly engaged teams.

If we expand on the first project—**Design and implement a competitive, market-informed benefits package that supports employee well-being and retention**—it can translate into several specific goals, such as:

1. Conducting external market research to benchmark benefits against industry standards.

2. Surveying employees to identify which benefits they value most.

3. Collaborating with benefits providers to design innovative, cost-effective offerings.

4. Developing a communication strategy to ensure employees understand and utilize their benefits.

These examples demonstrate how a high-level KRA can be broken down into actionable goals and initiatives. While the executive owns the strategic vision and direction, many of the supporting projects and tasks can be delegated to the team. A Key Result Area reflects work only you, as the leader, can own based on your expertise and perspective, while the execution often involves collaboration with others across your department.

Your KRAs may be impacted by the size of your organization, its resources, and its vision. For example, the board of directors of one organization may want the CEO to be involved in industry advocacy and legislation, but this may not be the expectation for a CEO at another organization.

TIPS TO DEFINE YOUR KEY RESULT AREAS

- Focus on results, not activities.

- Make sure your focus is high-level. Many leaders struggle to stay strategic and end up defining areas that are too tactical.

- Resist the urge to define too many areas. Keep the KRAs between 3–5. When you define them on paper, they may not seem like a lot. Yet, the focus of your Key Result Areas can be very complex. For example, "Strengthen workforce performance and engagement through strategic development initiatives, leadership capability building, and culture alignment" is a big job. This will entail several projects to achieve.

If you manage people, a core key result area should be coaching and developing your team to facilitate their best performance.

Leaders often struggle to prioritize this because they are too task-focused, but investing time in managing, coaching, and supporting your team is essential.

Can KRAs change? While they generally remain consistent unless a role significantly evolves, some organizations adjust them annually to align with strategic priorities. For example, for one of my manufacturing clients, a company-wide initiative to reduce waste by 10 percent was reflected as a key result area for all production employees.

Below are examples of Key Result Areas for different positions. This list is meant to spark ideas—your three to five KRAs will be specific to your role. It's not an exhaustive list of responsibilities, but rather examples to illustrate how KRAs might look in various positions.

FRONTLINE EMPLOYEE:

- **Customer/Member service associate:** Deliver exceptional customer or member service across all channels to enhance satisfaction and loyalty.
- **Payroll specialist:** Ensure accurate and timely processing of payroll to maintain employee trust and organizational compliance.

DEPARTMENT MANAGER:

- **Every management position:** Strengthen team performance by actively coaching, developing, and empowering each team member.
- **Accounting manager:** Ensure the financial health and integrity of the organization through sound budgeting, forecasting, and fiscal oversight.
- **Production manager:** Implement and sustain efficient workflows to3 maximize productivity and minimize manufacturing downtime.

EXECUTIVE LEADER:

- **Every executive position:** Analyze and anticipate industry trends to inform strategic planning and executive decision-making.
- **Chief operating officer:** Foster a culture of transparency and clarity by establishing strong communication systems between leadership, teams, and frontline employees.

Take a few minutes to define your KRAs. The more complex your role, the more challenging this exercise may be. Start with an initial list, refine it, and seek input from your manager to ensure alignment.

KEY RESULT AREAS EXERCISE

What are the Key Result Areas for your position?

1. _____
2. _____
3. _____
4. _____
5. _____

Once you've defined your KRAs, the next step is to assess how you're actually spending your time. Review your calendar. Are you prioritizing your KRAs, or are they getting lost in less important tasks? Many leaders either neglect their KRAs entirely or spend too little time on them.

This exercise can be extremely impactful for creating clarity around where you should be channeling your energy and focus to be most successful in your role. The goal is to shift your focus so that 80 percent of your time is spent on your KRAs, where you'll have the greatest impact. Ask yourself, "What do I need to let go of?" It might be attending every meeting instead of delegating to a team member, constantly checking email out of habit, or avoiding conversations about poor performance. Exceptional leaders minimize distractions and stay committed to their highest-value work.

What are three things you need to let go of or delegate so that you can focus on your KRAs?

1. _____

2. _____

3. _____

Once you have completed this exercise, I highly recommend that you have each of your direct reports define their KRAs. This exercise is a great way to create clarity and define expectations for each team member. It provides a structure for ensuring that you and your direct reports agree on Key Result Areas, allowing you to make adjustments. This ensures each employee has absolute clarity on where to focus their attention and energy.

POWER UP YOUR PRODUCTIVITY: THE FIVE MINUTE DAILY RESET

Once you've defined your Key Result Areas, the next step is aligning your daily actions with them. That alignment is built through intentional planning, starting with how you approach each day.

One simple yet powerful habit is taking just five minutes at the end of each workday to plan for the next. This small investment increases focus, momentum, and productivity. Without a clear plan, it's easy to get pulled into low-value tasks or start your morning feeling scattered and reactive.

Your Key Result Areas should guide how you spend your time—not just over the year or quarter, but each week, each day, and even hour by hour. Without that intentional approach, your time can easily be consumed by distractions, busywork, or reactive tasks that pull you away from creating impactful results.

Many professionals rely on to-do lists, but long lists often create decision fatigue and overwhelm. The more tasks on the list, the harder it becomes to focus on what truly matters. That's why identifying your top two priorities each day is so important. Instead of letting a long list run your day, decide what matters most, and block time for it on your calendar.

I've also found that this practice significantly reduces stress because it gives me a moment to recalibrate—to check in on what I accomplished, what I didn't, and what truly needs my focus moving forward. This simple habit makes me feel set up for success the next day, so I'm not lying in bed thinking about loose ends or feeling unnecessary anxiety. Taking five minutes to organize my thoughts and priorities allows me to step away from work with a clear mind, less stress, and confidence in the plan I've set for the next day.

Starting your morning with a clear plan eliminates decision fatigue, helps you hit the ground running, and ensures you're focused on what will produce the best results. A few minutes of planning the day before can save hours of wasted effort, setting you up for a productive, high-impact day.

SLOW DOWN TO SPEED UP

Most people believe that when they're behind, they need to speed up—work faster, put in longer hours, and push through exhaustion to catch up. But this approach often backfires, leading to more stress, scattered effort, and minimal progress. The real solution is counterintuitive: you need to slow down first.

By pausing to gain clarity on what truly matters, you can eliminate distractions and focus your energy on the right tasks—the ones that actually move the needle. Overwhelm isn't a sign that you need to do more; it's a sign that your priorities aren't clear. When you take the time to reset, refocus, and realign, you don't just get back on track; you create momentum that scattered effort could never achieve.

FOCUSING QUESTIONS

In moments of overwhelm, asking the right questions can shift you from scattered to focused—and help you regain control of your time and energy.

I first came across the concept of focusing questions in Gary Keller's book, *The One Thing*.[30] Inspired by his approach, I've adapted it into a simple yet powerful set of questions to create clarity in the planning process.

These questions can be applied to different time frames to help you prioritize effectively.

- What is the most important thing I should be working on this month?
- What is the most important thing I should be working on this week?
- What is the most important thing I should be working on today?
- What is the most important thing I should be working on right now?

These questions serve as both a big-picture guide and a moment-to-moment decision filter, helping you focus on what truly matters at every level. They act as a compass for your next move, ensuring you're always working on the highest-impact task.

Whenever I feel overwhelmed, it's almost always because I lack clarity on where to focus. With so much competing for my attention, my mind becomes overloaded, and I end up spinning my wheels. I've trained myself to pause and ask:

What is the most important thing I should be working on right now?

Not the easiest task, not the one I feel like doing—*the most important*. This one question instantly cuts through the noise and gives me the clarity I need to take meaningful action.

Multi-Tasking Kills Productivity

Despite what many leaders believe, multitasking is a productivity killer.[31] Research shows that our brains aren't designed to focus on multiple complex tasks at once.[32] Instead of getting more done, we end up juggling too many things poorly, leading to mistakes, stress, and diminished quality. Studies estimate that multitasking can reduce productivity by up to 40 percent and costs businesses $450 billion annually in lost efficiency.[33]

Yet, multitasking remains a prized skill in many workplaces, even highlighted as a sought-after skill in job descriptions and position advertisements. In reality, the obsession with squeezing more into every minute only creates overload, scattered attention, and burnout. The solution is intentional single-tasking. Choose one priority, commit your full attention to it, and execute it with excellence. As a manager, you need to stay on top of multiple projects and priorities, but trying to juggle more than one task at a time can pull your focus and reduce effectiveness. True productivity is not about juggling everything at once.

Letting go of multitasking takes a shift in mindset, especially in fast-paced environments where constant responsiveness is the norm. But when everything feels urgent, nothing is truly prioritized. Single-tasking gives you the ability to reclaim your focus and direct your energy to what matters most. It means turning off distractions, protecting your time, and giving yourself permission to slow down in order to move forward with greater clarity. Leaders who embrace this approach make better decisions, produce higher quality work, and experience less burnout—because they are not just busy, they are effective.

COMPRESSING TIME

Even with better focus, many leaders still feel overwhelmed. That is because the issue often is not effort; it is how time is being spent.

Most leaders feel overworked and exhausted, not because they lack effort, but because they spend their time on the wrong things. To catch up, they extend their work hours, yet the opposite effect occurs: productivity declines the more we work. Adding hours to the day isn't the solution; it's a sign of inefficiency.

While occasional extra hours may be necessary for major projects, consistently overworking is a clear sign of inefficiency and a lack of prioritization. Busyness is often mistaken for progress, but meaningful leadership is about focused execution and purposeful results, not endless hours.

One of the most effective ways to boost productivity is to compress your work hours. That's right—working *less*, not more, often leads to greater efficiency. This doesn't mean cutting your workload in half, but rather setting clear boundaries. Work expands to fit the time we allow it, just like meetings that drag on because they were scheduled for an hour. Setting a firm stop time increases your focus and forces greater intentionality with how you use your day.

Stanford University research confirms that productivity per hour drops sharply after 50 hours of work per week.[34] By setting limits on your workday, you'll use your time more wisely, achieve better results, and have more energy for the next day. Start by ending your day just 30 minutes earlier, and notice how much more focused and effective you become. If you've been working long hours and still feel like you're not as productive as you could be, this small shift can be a powerful first step. You can begin with 30 minutes and gradually work toward a more reasonable end time that supports both your performance and well-being. The purpose is to shift away from chronic overwork and move toward a more intentional, sustainable schedule.

Compressed time isn't only about the length of your workday; it's just as powerful when applied to how you structure meetings.

One of my clients recently shared a simple but powerful shift: They stopped defaulting to 60-minute meetings and started scheduling them for 25, 40, or 50 minutes instead. Not only has this helped people stay more focused during the meeting, but it also creates space between meetings, giving everyone a much-needed buffer to reset and refocus. This small shift creates breathing room and leads to more focused, productive meetings.

PRODUCTIVITY SPRINTS: THE KEY TO DEEP FOCUS AND HIGH PERFORMANCE

When your day is filled with shifting priorities and nonstop demands, it's easy to stay busy while making little real progress. The solution to scattered, unproductive days is productivity sprints: dedicated, distraction-free work blocks that dramatically increase efficiency. Research shows that constantly switching tasks can make work take up to 500 percent longer.[35] By breaking large tasks into smaller parts, scheduling focused time in your calendar, and eliminating distractions—closing your email, silencing notifications, and setting clear boundaries—you create an intentional space for results.

Many leaders misinterpret an "open door policy" as a need to be constantly available, but that level of accessibility kills focus and drains productivity. I believe the original intention behind the open-door policy was to encourage approachability, openness, and support, not to suggest that a leader should be available at all times. Unfortunately, the phrase has been taken too literally in many organizations.

We need to stop using the term altogether. It sends the wrong message and creates unrealistic expectations for leaders who are already stretched thin. Instead, leaders should model a culture of accessibility with boundaries. Being available for your team is important, but so is protecting time for deep work, strategic thinking, and follow-through.

The solution is to set clear expectations. Let your team know when you're stepping into a period of focused work. Say something like, "I'll be working on a project for the next 90 minutes. If it's urgent, you can interrupt; otherwise, I'll be available at 1:00." This approach maintains trust and approachability while signaling that focused time matters.

When leaders respect their own time and protect their focus, they model those behaviors for their teams, fostering a culture that values deep work and prioritizes meaningful results.

Your environment plays a powerful role in focus and energy. If you're constantly interrupted, your office might be the least effective place to do focused work. A simple change of scenery can help increase clarity and focus. As a vice president, I would often go to a coffee shop to work on important projects. I would accomplish more in two hours at a coffee shop than I would in an entire week at the office. Even now, I often leave my home office and work in my basement so I can focus on one thing and not be distracted. Another option is reserving a quiet conference room and bringing only the project you're working on—no distractions, no inbox, just focused progress.

Productivity sprints are effective for both Key Result Areas and routine tasks. Even checking email is more efficient when done in scheduled blocks rather than throughout the day. When you plan ahead and commit to productivity sprints, you'll accomplish more in less time, transforming both your effectiveness and success.

According to McKinsey, the average employee is interrupted 50–60 times per day, with 80 percent of those interruptions being unimportant.[36] This constant disruption pulls professionals out of the flow state, where they can be five times more productive—and this study focused on employees, not leaders![37] The issue isn't just external interruptions; nearly half of all disruptions are self-inflicted.[38] This means that almost half of our distractions come from checking our phone, stopping to check email, or engaging in multitasking behaviors.

No wonder we struggle to get meaningful work done! To maximize productivity sprints, eliminate as many distractions as possible—put away electronic devices, close your email, and create an environment where you can focus deeply. I promise that if you consistently implement this practice, you will see dramatic results in your focus and productivity.

CONTROLLING INTERRUPTIONS: KEEPING FOCUS IN A DISTRACTED WORKPLACE

Workplace interruptions take a serious toll on productivity and well-being. Research from the University of California, Irvine, found that office workers are interrupted roughly every 12 minutes and 40 seconds, and it takes an average of 25 minutes and 26 seconds to refocus on the original task.[39] These constant disruptions accumulate throughout the day, yet many leaders accept them as an unavoidable part of the job.

While eliminating interruptions entirely isn't realistic, reducing them can dramatically improve focus, efficiency, and strategic thinking. Ironically, the most approachable managers, those who build strong relationships, often experience more frequent interruptions.

Employees feel comfortable dropping in with "quick questions" or seeking input, often out of convenience rather than necessity.

When I worked at the credit union, my team regularly asked me questions they could have answered using available resources, simply because it was faster to pop into my office. Over time, these minor disruptions compound, draining productivity, increasing stress, and extending work hours. Worse, they foster dependency, preventing employees from developing the critical problem-solving skills they need. While some interruptions are necessary, most are not urgent, and learning to manage them is key to a more effective workplace.

Here are a few ways to communicate boundaries and manage interruptions while remaining supportive.

- "I'm in full focus mode and making great progress on a project right now. Can you schedule something on my calendar for later today?"
- "I have about two minutes right now. If you need more time, let's schedule something later."
- "I'm closing my door to focus on a major project. I'll be available at 1:00 unless it's urgent."
- "I'm heading to a conference room to work on an important project. I can be reached on my cell phone, if necessary."

By setting clear expectations, you protect your time, boost productivity, and encourage your team to develop independence—all without sacrificing approachability.

PRIORITY PLANNING: A STRATEGIC APPROACH TO GETTING RESULTS

It's human nature to procrastinate on big, important tasks in favor of smaller, easier ones. We often fill our days with busy work—checking emails, attending meetings, answering calls—then try to squeeze in meaningful projects around them. Instead of setting our own agenda, we let emails and calendar invites dictate our time.

I learned this the hard way. Five years into my business, things were going great. My calendar was full with clients, and my business was growing. But by June, I realized I hadn't scheduled a single vacation. Looking ahead, there wasn't a single week left in the year without a commitment. The best I could manage was a long weekend; there was no room for a real vacation. By the end of the year, I felt overworked, depleted, and stressed. From that moment on, I committed to scheduling my vacations before the year even begins. Now, I not only plan my time off in advance, but I also book and pay for trips early, making sure they actually happen.

Effective leadership doesn't happen by chance; it requires intentional planning. That means proactively scheduling your highest priorities—both professional and personal—so they're reflected in your calendar, not just your to-do list. I use a process I call *Priority Planning*, which ensures that KRAs, strategic meetings, and even vacations are scheduled first. Everything else is arranged around them.

This approach can feel counterintuitive, especially when a long list of tasks is calling for your attention. But if you spend all your time reacting to what's urgent, you'll never create space for what's most important. Real progress happens when you protect time for the work that creates results.

Priority Planning is a key strategy for highly effective leaders, ensuring that essential key results are intentionally scheduled and prioritized rather than squeezed in around less critical tasks. The key is not to wait—successful leaders proactively block time for their most important priorities before their calendar fills up. I've found the best time to do this is before the new year begins, entering all major commitments in advance, but you can start at any time to take control of your schedule and focus on what truly matters.

Tips for Priority Planning

1. Schedule your vacations and other time off before the beginning of the year.
2. Schedule regular "strategy days" or "planning days" in your calendar.

3. Schedule time each week for planning and preparation.

4. Schedule recurring team meetings in your calendar.

5. When starting a new project, schedule recurring time in your calendar to complete its phases or tasks.

6. When leading a project, schedule all project meetings with key stakeholders at the start of the project. This ensures that all project team members have the meetings prioritized on their calendars and eliminates the need to figure out everyone's schedule each time you need to meet.

7. Schedule 60 to 90-minute daily productivity sprints in your calendar, preferably in the morning or your peak energy times for the best focus.

8. Schedule recurring coaching sessions with each of your staff members before the year starts.

9. Schedule time to read industry news or research strategies and best practices in your industry.

10. Schedule doctor appointments, your children's important events, and other important personal time before the year begins.

11. Decide on the conferences and industry events you want to attend, register for them, and schedule them in your calendar.

What will you Priority Plan into your schedule?

1. _____

2. _____

3. _____

4. _____

Asking for Clarity

Throughout this chapter, we've explored personal productivity strategies, but I want to close with one of the most impactful habits leaders at every level should adopt: asking for clarity. If we normalize seeking clarity across the organization, we can drastically reduce wasted time, misaligned efforts, and unnecessary stress caused by confusion.

When you're uncertain about your role, responsibilities, deadlines, or next steps, take ownership by asking for clarification. Even at the leadership level, it's essential to seek clarity when expectations are vague. This not only ensures alignment but also sets the tone for your team, demonstrating that asking questions is a sign of professionalism and ownership, not weakness. When employees feel empowered to seek clarity, everyone moves forward with confidence toward strategic goals.

The reality is, even at the executive level, clarity is often lacking. I've worked with countless organizations where leaders themselves struggle to articulate the company's strategic priorities for the year. In fact, I'd bet that if I asked every executive in most organizations to name the top strategic priorities, more than 85 percent would have difficulty answering. Too often, leadership teams spend time crafting a great strategic plan in an off-site retreat, only to return to business as usual, without a structured way to revisit or communicate those priorities throughout the organization. The result? Misalignment, wasted effort, and a workforce unsure of where to focus.

No matter your position, asking for clarity is a proactive way to take ownership and achieve success. If you feel overwhelmed by competing priorities or an excessive workload, initiating a conversation with your manager can help bring focus and ensure alignment. For example, when given a new assignment while already managing multiple projects, you might say:

"This project sounds important. I'm currently working on Projects A, B, and C—can you help me prioritize which is most critical right now?"

This isn't about challenging authority or avoiding responsibility; it's about making informed decisions and ensuring the most important work gets done effectively. Leaders don't always have full visibility into everything competing for your time, so offering context helps them set clearer expectations and make smarter decisions.

Here are a few simple yet powerful ways to seek clarity.

- "When do you need this by?"
- "Can you give me an example to help clarify what you need?"
- "What is the expected outcome?"
- "What specifically do you need from me?"

Encouraging clarity at all levels—from frontline employees to senior leaders—ensures that people can take action with confidence, reducing inefficiencies and communication gaps.

Being a leader also means serving as a strategic advisor to your manager. That includes asking thoughtful questions, seeking clarity, and being upfront about the implications of taking on additional work. This perspective helps protect team capacity, align resources, and ensure that effort is directed toward the organization's highest priorities. For example, you might say:

"We don't have the capacity on the team to take on a new project without shifting what we are currently working on. Would you like to review our current priorities together so we can create alignment on how to move forward?"

By framing the conversation this way, you're not pushing back—you're protecting results, supporting your team, and helping your manager make informed, strategic decisions for the good of the organization.

I hope this chapter has inspired you to be more intentional with your energy, focus, and time, not just in your work, but in your life. Clarity isn't just about productivity; it's about ensuring that your efforts lead to meaningful results. As a leader, your responsibility is not only to create clarity for yourself by focusing on key priorities and managing your attention, but also to ensure your team has the clarity they need to stay aligned and achieve results. In the next chapter, I'll share strategies for communicating effectively with your team and ensuring they stay focused on their most important priorities.

11

LEADING WITH CLARITY—THE KEY TO EFFECTIVE COMMUNICATION AND TEAM ALIGNMENT

Leadership is the capacity to translate vision into reality.

—Warren Bennis

One of a leader's most essential responsibilities is creating clarity. Your role is to communicate the organization's purpose and goals in a way that resonates, helping your team see their connection to the bigger picture. When people understand how their work contributes to the broader vision, they feel more engaged and empowered to take action.

In today's digital world, employees are overwhelmed by a constant influx of information while juggling strategic projects, daily tasks, and shifting priorities. This overload makes it harder to focus and absorb key messages. Research shows that after just one day, people retain only about 33 percent of what they hear.[40] Yet many leaders communicate a message once and assume it sticks. In reality, reinforcing key messages through multiple channels significantly improves retention and alignment.

Without clear and consistent communication, teams become misaligned, time is wasted, and productivity suffers. In the absence of information, people fill in the gaps with their own assumptions—assumptions that are often inaccurate. Misunderstandings breed confusion, unnecessary work, and even distrust, all of which derail progress.

Leaders must *continually* create clarity, especially in a fast-paced, constantly evolving environment where priorities frequently shift. Teams can only remain agile when goals, expectations, and direction are clearly defined and consistently reinforced.

WHAT'S YOUR MOVIE?

Several years ago, I asked one of my team members to order books for two upcoming leadership programs and told her to place the orders separately, since I planned to bill one client directly. What I *meant* was to place two separate orders—15 books in each. What I *said* wasn't clear. She ended up placing 15 individual orders for one client. It was a perfect example of me knowing exactly what I meant, but failing to communicate it effectively.

As someone who is fast-paced and action-oriented, I've learned that I sometimes skip over important details or assume others understand what's in my head. To avoid misunderstandings like this, I now pause to confirm clarity before moving forward. I'll often ask a quick follow-up like, "I'm not always the best at articulating what's in my head. Can you share what you heard so I can make sure I included all the key details?"

By framing it this way, I take responsibility for the clarity of my message rather than making it seem like I'm testing the other person's understanding, which could come across as condescending.

When we communicate, we often have a vivid "movie" playing in our minds—a detailed mental picture of what we want to convey. The problem is that we forget others can't see the same film. We have all the context, backstory, and details in our heads, but we don't always share the key information others need to fully understand the message.

Imagine walking into a movie theater 30 minutes late. You've missed the critical opening scenes that set the stage for the story. Without that foundation, the plot feels disjointed and confusing.

Leaders often communicate this way, leaving out key context and details that are important for others to take action effectively and achieve the desired results. This leads to misunderstandings, misaligned efforts, and wasted time.

To lead effectively, we need to "play the full movie" for our teams. That means breaking down the scenes, providing the necessary background and details, and clearly painting the picture we see. When we do, we eliminate confusion, build alignment, and empower others to take action with clarity and purpose.

CLARITY FRAMEWORK FOR ASSIGNING TASKS

When delegating tasks or projects, providing complete and clear information is essential for setting employees up for success. Many leaders focus only on what needs to be done, while overlooking the equally important why it matters and when it is due. Without this context, employees may struggle to prioritize or fully understand the purpose behind their work.

To ensure clarity and effectiveness, always communicate:

- **Why** the task is important.
- **What** specifically needs to be done.
- **When** it must be completed.

Equally important is creating space for questions and confirming understanding.

Delegation is not a one-way conversation; it is a two-way exchange of information and responsibilities. Encourage employees to ask clarifying questions, share concerns, or suggest alternative approaches. This not only promotes alignment and ownership but also helps uncover any gaps in communication that might have been missed. When leaders ensure mutual understanding, they build greater accountability, confidence, and performance, turning delegation into a strategic opportunity for growth rather than just a transfer of tasks.

THE POWER OF DELEGATION: LETTING GO TO LEVEL UP

Delegation is more than just a way to lighten your workload; it is a cornerstone of effective leadership. When done well, it creates the time and space you need to focus on the most important areas of results and impact. As a manager, your role is not to do everything yourself, but to achieve outcomes through others. Delegation is how you scale your impact, develop your team, and ensure the long-term success of your department or organization.

Yet many leaders struggle with letting go. They hold onto tasks and projects either out of habit, a desire for control, or a belief that it's simply faster to do it themselves. But this mindset is a trap. Under-delegating is one of the most common leadership pitfalls, and it can severely limit your effectiveness. Leaders who fail to delegate often find themselves overwhelmed, bogged down in the weeds, and unable to focus on higher-level thinking and strategy.

In fact, lack of delegation is one of the Six Leadership Saboteurs that undermine leadership effectiveness. Many managers fall into this trap by clinging to tasks they performed in a previous role or staying overly focused on the technical side of the work. There are several reasons leaders struggle to delegate.

- **Fear of giving up control:** They believe they can do it better or faster, or they don't fully trust their team to deliver.

- **Tying their value to technical expertise:** Instead of evolving into a strategic leader, they stay stuck in execution, where they feel useful and competent.

- **Protecting their team:** Some managers are afraid to overwhelm employees and keep work that would actually help others grow.

- **Lack of delegation skills:** Many simply haven't been taught how to delegate effectively—how to assign work with clarity, context, and the right level of support.

But holding onto tasks for any of these reasons doesn't serve anyone in the long run. It keeps leaders stuck in reactive mode, limits team growth, and creates a bottleneck in productivity. Delegation done well is not just a practical necessity; it's a leadership imperative.

To delegate effectively, start by considering the strengths and talents of your team. Match tasks and projects to individuals based on what they're good at and what they aspire to do more of. It might take more time initially to train, coach, or mentor someone through a new responsibility, but that investment pays off. Over time, you'll find yourself needing to spend less time on the task, while your employee gains valuable experience and ownership.

Delegation is not about dumping work; it's about developing people. The most effective leaders understand that letting go is not a loss of control, but a strategic approach that builds a stronger, more capable team.

One of the negative delegation habits I consistently have to work on is what I call Drive by Delegation. Drive by Delegation is when you assign a task on the fly, often without enough context, clarity, or follow-up, leaving the other person unsure of expectations. As someone who moves quickly and likes to keep projects in motion, I have to be very intentional about slowing down and clearly thinking through what I am delegating. A few years ago, I asked my executive assistant, Lisa, to research web development companies because our website was outdated and needed a refresh. I knew I wanted something more modern and relevant, so I asked her at a very general level to start researching. What I did not do was provide any structure, goals, or criteria for what I meant by "refresh."

A couple of weeks later, Lisa came back and asked for more clarity. She had started the research, but with thousands of options of web designers, she needed more direction from me on what I was looking for in a web designer. In my rush to get the project going and off my plate, I skipped the most important part: providing her with the context and details she needed to do the job effectively. At that moment, I realized I was not setting her up for success. By keeping my instructions general, I was hindering her ability to do the job well.

Dr. Brene Brown says, "Clear is kind, unclear is unkind."[41] My interaction with Lisa is an excellent example of how a lack of clarity does not support an employee's success. Lisa wanted to do great work, but without the necessary details, she was left guessing and unsure if she was meeting expectations. That experience made me realize that Drive by Delegation does not save time. It creates confusion, delays, and frustration for the team member who is trying their best to succeed. I still have to be mindful of this to ensure I am not delegating too quickly. I make a conscious effort to slow down, think through what success looks like, and communicate with clarity so that my team has what they need to deliver great results.

Delegation is not just about moving something off your plate; it is about setting someone else up to confidently take ownership of the project or task.

One of the most common reasons leaders avoid delegation is that they feel they do not have the time. It often seems easier to just do something that will take five or ten minutes rather than taking 45 minutes to train someone else. In the short term, this makes sense—it feels more efficient to knock it out yourself. But in the long term, this habit keeps leaders stuck in the weeds, constantly focused on low-value tasks instead of important key result areas. The work may get done, but at the cost of caretaking the culture, strategic execution, and team development.

To break this cycle, I have implemented a simple but effective practice: creating a delegation list. Throughout the week, whenever I catch myself doing a task that would be better suited for someone else, I write it on my delegation list. This serves as an ongoing list of tasks that I should not handle personally. I may not delegate everything at once, but this list helps me be more intentional about shifting responsibilities over time. Instead of defaulting to doing it myself, I can prioritize what to delegate based on what will free up my time and develop my team.

One of the most impactful lessons I have learned about delegation comes from Dan Sullivan, CEO of Strategic Coach®. He teaches a simple but powerful shift in thinking: when faced with a new project or task, instead of asking, *How will I do this?* ask, *Who on my team can handle this?*[42] This shift—from *How* to *Who*—is a fundamental mindset change that allows leaders to facilitate results through others, rather than taking on everything themselves.

When you learn to delegate effectively, you stay focused on your Key Result Areas, ultimately facilitating results through others while ensuring you have the time and capacity to focus on the strategic aspects of leadership that often get neglected when you're stuck in the weeds—coaching your team, fostering collaboration, and making high-impact decisions.

Dan also shares a powerful delegation framework that ensures clarity and success.[43]

1. **Purpose:** Clearly define the purpose of the project or task. What do you want to accomplish? Why is this important?
2. **Ideal Outcome:** Paint a clear picture of what success looks like. What does the completed project look like? How will you know it is done well?
3. **Success Criteria:** Set the benchmarks for success. What has to be true when the project is finished? What key elements or standards need to be met?

Applying this framework, along with the delegation list, has helped me slow down and delegate with more intentionality. Instead of simply handing off tasks, I now ensure my team has the clarity and direction they need to succeed. Delegation is not just about getting work done; it's about building capability, trust, and results through others.

Effective delegation is a powerful tool for achieving results through others, but it is only one piece of effective leadership. To truly support your team and ensure alignment, you need consistent communication. One-on-one and team meetings provide the structure for reinforcing expectations, clarifying priorities, and addressing any challenges, providing the alignment and direction necessary for achieving results.

Using One-on-One and Team Meetings to Create Clarity

Not all meetings are productive, but when structured effectively, regular one-on-one and team meetings are powerful tools for reinforcing goals, keeping employees focused, addressing challenges, and ensuring alignment. Whether in person or virtual, these meetings provide a dedicated space for discussion, problem-solving, and coaching.

Some leaders view regular meetings as a waste of time, and they certainly can be if not run well. However, leaders who lack a consistent forum to track progress on goals often lose visibility into what their teams are working on and miss the opportunity to gain clarity, remove obstacles, and provide needed support. Employees, in turn, can become disconnected, overwhelmed, and uncertain about priorities. Meetings don't need to be long; in fact, shorter meetings often encourage preparation, focus, and efficiency.

Asking open-ended questions encourages engagement, ensures employees understand key tasks, and helps leaders provide coaching that facilitates better results.

Consider using these questions to spark meaningful discussions and reinforce clarity.

- What is your biggest challenge right now?
- What is the next step?
- What needs to happen to ensure this project is a success?
- Which other departments should be involved in this process?
- What questions do you have?
- What concerns should we address?
- Are there any gaps we might be missing?
- Based on what I just shared, what do you see as the top three takeaways?
- What are your top three priorities this week?

You may not ask all of these questions in a single meeting, but taking just five minutes at the end of your one-on-one and team meetings can significantly enhance clarity, alignment, and accountability. In the *Caretake the Culture* chapter, I'll share additional coaching questions you can use during meetings to guide more effective employee conversations.

One-on-one meetings are one of the most valuable tools a leader has, but too often, they become bogged down by task updates or status check-ins. While staying aligned on progress is important, using this time solely to review to-do lists is a missed opportunity. Instead, one-on-ones should be used to coach through challenges, provide clarity, and delegate with intention. These conversations are a chance to support your employee's growth, strengthen alignment, and ensure they have what they need to move forward confidently. Shifting the focus from task sharing to strategic dialogue makes one-on-ones more effective, more purposeful, and far more impactful for both the leader and the employee.

In my one-on-one meetings with team members, we often spend the majority of our time focused on something I'm delegating or coaching them through, rather than reviewing a list of completed tasks. This approach is a much more valuable use of our time. We use a shared document to track task updates and progress, which allows us to stay informed without needing to use meeting time to go through every detail. Instead, we can focus on where the employee needs clarity, support, or guidance to move forward effectively.

Clarity is essential to effective leadership, providing the direction and alignment teams need to stay focused and create results. Without it, priorities become blurred, teams lose momentum, and progress slows. Yet in today's world, where priorities can shift overnight and new information constantly reshapes our path, you won't always have absolute clarity. Leaders must be able to adapt, navigate uncertainty, and manage the tension between the need for clarity and the reality of ambiguity.

Leaders must also create an environment where people feel supported, valued, and motivated to do their best work. This leads to the next key element, caretaking the culture, where we will explore how leaders can build a strong workplace that fosters engagement, trust, and long-term success.

12

CARETAKE THE CULTURE

It is better to know some of the
questions than all of the answers.

—James Thurber

The role of a leader has shifted. In today's dynamic workplace, performance isn't driven by title or power; it's driven by presence, purpose, and the ability to connect and adapt. Gone are the days when leadership was about giving orders and expecting compliance. The most effective leaders understand that success comes from connection, coaching, consistent feedback, and employee development. Modern leadership requires a relational approach—one that prioritizes engagement, growth, and a thriving team culture.

In the traditional leadership model, relational aspects were often undervalued. Leaders were seen as decision makers and problem solvers—fixers who gave orders and expected results. While this approach worked in the past, it's no longer effective in today's workplace. Many of us were trained in this environment and reported to managers who embodied this model, which makes the shift to modern leadership especially challenging. Success is now measured not just by completing tasks but by fostering engagement, building thriving teams, and creating career development opportunities. As society has evolved and new generations have entered the workforce, employee expectations have shifted. People want leaders who facilitate growth, provide meaningful opportunities, and invest in their development, not just direct and correct.

To be an exceptional leader today requires a shift from a more technical focus on fixing, telling, and directing to facilitating results through influence, connection, and coaching. This means moving away from a "fixer" mindset—where leaders spend their time solving problems for employees—and embracing the role of a facilitator. Facilitators don't just provide answers; they develop their teams through coaching, feedback, support, and connection. They create environments where employees are empowered to take ownership, innovate, and make meaningful contributions to the organization's success.

The Power of Engagement

Employees want to feel a sense of fulfillment and growth in their work, and this requires leaders who are intentional, communicative, and invested in their development. A highly engaged workforce is a powerful driver of organizational success, yet as I mentioned in the beginning of this book, according to Gallup, only 31 percent of employees are engaged at work, which is at a decade low as of this writing.[44] Engagement typically hovers between 31 and 34 percent, highlighting a significant opportunity for organizations.

Creating an environment where employees want to bring their full mental, physical, and emotional energy to work each day leads to higher productivity, better business results, and thriving teams. When leaders make engagement a priority, they cultivate a culture where employees feel valued, empowered, and inspired to do their best work. They recognize and reward achievements, encourage collaboration, and cultivate open communication. These intentional efforts don't just boost morale; they fuel performance and drive lasting business success.

FROM DOING WORK TO LEADING PEOPLE

Caretaking the Culture is a vital component of exceptional leadership, and leaders should dedicate significant time and energy to it. However, many managers find this aspect challenging. It's often easier to focus on the technical side of the job—checking tasks off a list—than to invest in relationships and build a strong team culture.

Effective leadership is active, not passive. It's not just about the position you occupy, it's about the actions you take every day. Passive leadership often looks like waiting for problems to surface, assuming your team knows what's expected without clear direction, or stepping back until something goes wrong. Active leadership, on the other hand, means being engaged and intentional—setting expectations, checking in regularly, offering feedback, coaching through a challenge, and showing appreciation.

Many managers mistake constant activity for meaningful leadership. They stay busy responding to emails, handling last-minute issues, or sitting in meetings, yet overlook the actions that truly strengthen teams. Leading well requires consistent, deliberate effort and creating an environment where your team can thrive and perform at their best.

By shifting from simply getting things done to fostering engagement and development, you will amplify your influence and impact and accelerate results on your team. I refer to this as *Caretaking the Culture*—one of the three pillars of exceptional leadership. It's the people-centered side of leadership that's essential for success today: building trust, alignment, and a focus on both individual and team growth.

FOSTERING PSYCHOLOGICAL SAFETY

At the heart of Caretaking the Culture is fostering psychological safety, creating an environment where employees feel comfortable speaking up, sharing their perspectives, and contributing without fear of judgment or retaliation. When people trust that their ideas and feedback matter, collaboration and innovation flourish. Beyond psychological safety, leaders must actively shape the culture by building genuine connections, showing appreciation, providing consistent and meaningful feedback, coaching and developing employees, and addressing challenges to keep the team strong and resilient. Culture is not something that takes care of itself. It must be consistently cultivated. It is the daily actions of a leader, recognizing efforts, offering guidance, encouraging growth, and ensuring open communication, that create an environment where employees feel valued, supported, and inspired to do their best work.

The most important elements of Caretaking the Culture are connection, appreciation and recognition, feedback, coaching and developing, and addressing challenges. They are all grounded in the foundation of psychological safety. Essentially, it's about cultivating a healthy team environment that enables everyone to thrive.

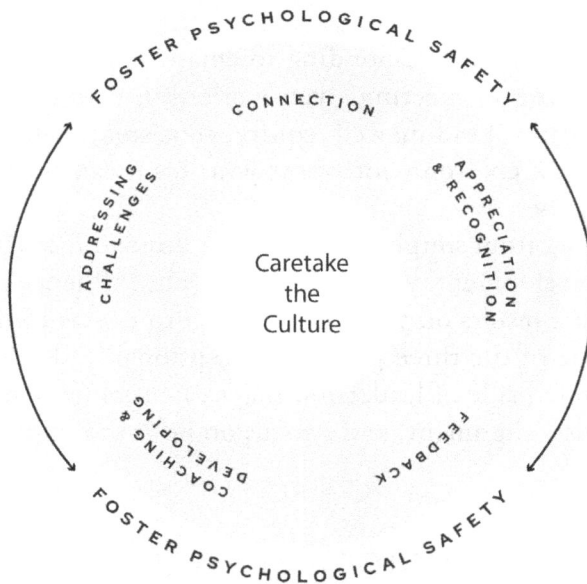

According to Gallup, only 21 percent of US employees strongly agree that they trust the leadership of their organization.[45] There are many ways executives and managers can build a culture of trust, and one of the most important elements is fostering psychological safety.

Even the most approachable and supportive managers must be intentional about fostering psychological safety, as some employees may still hesitate to share their true opinions or perspectives simply because of the inherent power dynamic. As a manager, your position of authority can make it challenging for employees to speak openly, making it essential to create an environment where they feel genuinely safe to express themselves.

Building psychological safety in the workplace is crucial for fostering a culture of trust, collaboration, and innovation. Here are some key strategies you can use to cultivate psychological safety.

1. **Encourage constructive conflict.** Many leaders view all conflict as negative, but constructive conflict is both necessary and healthy for high-performing teams. Managers should encourage healthy conflict by asking for differing points of view. Many teams hover more toward artificial harmony, where employees don't speak up and go along with decisions to preserve harmony, even when they disagree. Both destructive conflict and artificial harmony are toxic to teams because they don't foster an environment where employees can speak their minds without fear of consequences. Even in very positive cultures, employees may hold back out of fear of going against the positive narrative, so it's important for leaders in all organizations to foster psychological safety and encourage constructive conflict.

2. **When possible, listen before you share.** When a leader shares their ideas first in a meeting, employees will often agree because they want to preserve the relationship or don't feel comfortable disagreeing with their boss. Try to solicit ideas from team members before you share your perspective to surface different ideas and opinions.

3. **Actively invite differing opinions.** It's not enough to just ask what team members think. To foster psychological safety, use specific questions and statements that encourage constructive conflict. For example:

    a. Who has an idea that is different from the ones already shared?

    b. I'd like to hear from someone who disagrees.

    c. I'm open to feedback on this. Tell me why and how my idea won't work.

    d. Who has a different view on this topic?

This not only encourages different perspectives and constructive conflict, but it also normalizes differing views and demonstrates that leaders expect employees to disagree.

4. **Acknowledge opposing views.** When an employee has the courage to disagree with you or a colleague in a constructive way, acknowledge it. This fosters a sense of safety; employees will feel more comfortable disagreeing and sharing their true ideas and opinions because you have demonstrated that these differing viewpoints are welcome. For example, "Jane, I appreciate you sharing that you disagree with the direction we have been discussing for this project." Even if you don't agree with the employee's view, you can still acknowledge them for speaking up.

5. **Regularly check in with each individual and your team.** Go beyond using your individual and team meetings for only discussing tasks and projects. A few times a year, take the opportunity to go deeper by asking questions that strengthen working relationships. This is a powerful exercise to use one-on-one *and* with your full team.

    a. What is working well?

    b. What is not working well?

    c. How can I support you better?

    d. How can the team support you better?

Give people time to reflect on these questions before the discussion, which will lead to more thoughtful responses and a better conversation. When you let your team know that these conversations will be a regular part of how you work together, you normalize open feedback and continuous improvement. Over time, this builds trust and encourages employees to speak up, share ideas, and help shape a more effective and collaborative team environment.

6. **Model accountability.** One of the best and most important ways to build a culture of trust and authenticity is to ensure that your words and actions align. People don't follow what you say; they follow what you do. It's often the small things that chip away at trust and integrity. Following through on even the small things also builds trust, accountability, and psychological safety. Model accountability in your everyday actions—be on time, follow through with commitments, and admit mistakes. When employees see their leader not only do what they say, but also admit when they make mistakes, they are more likely to do the same.

> PEOPLE DON'T FOLLOW WHAT YOU SAY; THEY FOLLOW WHAT YOU DO.

Creating psychological safety on your team and in your culture takes consistent focus and intention. The healthiest cultures build practices at every leadership level to solicit the real truth from employees. By providing a safe space to surface issues, challenges, and differing ideas, you foster a healthy, thriving organizational culture.

CONNECTED LEADERSHIP: CULTIVATING STRONG RELATIONSHIPS

When Frank Blake, former CEO of Home Depot, retired in 2014, employees flooded him with handwritten notes of appreciation. Over his seven-year tenure, Blake estimated that he had personally written over 25,000 handwritten notes to associates.[46] This simple yet powerful habit not only strengthened connections but also left a lasting impact on his influence and legacy as a leader. It serves as a great reminder that small, intentional acts of appreciation can have a profound effect on workplace culture.

One of the most essential aspects of nurturing a strong culture, fostering engagement, and building a thriving team is creating genuine connections. Leaders must go beyond managing tasks to build meaningful relationships with their team members, understanding their unique strengths, motivations, and aspirations. When leaders take the time to connect on a personal level, they create a sense of belonging and loyalty that fosters a positive, high-performing work environment.

Building connections doesn't require sharing every detail of your personal life or knowing everything about your employees' lives. You can be a private leader and still foster meaningful relationships by showing genuine interest, listening, and authentically engaging with your team.

The most effective way to strengthen relationships is to show genuine interest in each individual and make time for personal interactions. While there are many ways to build connections, simple yet impactful practices include engaging in team activities, walking around to check in with employees, recognizing achievements with a handwritten note or thoughtful email, and creating a fun and supportive workplace culture.

By incorporating intentional and consistent connection-building practices, leaders can enhance trust, collaboration, and overall team cohesion. One of my favorite ways to foster camaraderie is by beginning meetings with a brief connection exercise. I integrate these into every leadership workshop I facilitate, and they have proven to be an effective way to deepen mutual understanding and build lasting relationships among team members.

- **High/Low:** Each person takes a moment to share one high point (a success, achievement, or positive experience) and one low point (a challenge, setback, or difficulty) from the past couple of weeks. This can be personal or professional.

- **Bucket List Exercise:** Give employees a few minutes to write down items from their bucket list—things they hope to experience or achieve. Each person shares one or two, sparking conversation and helping team members learn more about each other.

- **One Word:** Each team member shares one word that describes how they feel in the moment, offering quick insight into their mindset. Leaders can follow up on responses that stand out, showing care and strengthening team awareness.

- **New or Good:** Each person shares something new or good from the past two weeks, whether personal or professional. This simple exercise fosters gratitude, optimism, and team connection.

These opening exercises are especially valuable for remote teams, where casual office interactions don't naturally occur. Managers need to be intentional about fostering connections by consistently creating opportunities for meaningful conversations, such as virtual coffee conversations, informal check-ins, or teambuilding activities.

A powerful method for strengthening relationships is to show genuine interest in employees' personal and professional goals and to actively provide feedback, coaching, and guidance to help them achieve these goals.

APPRECIATION AND RECOGNITION

Appreciation and recognition are fundamental to Caretaking the Culture because they help create a positive and motivated team. When employees feel valued for their contributions, it not only boosts morale but also strengthens their commitment to the organization's goals. Regular recognition reinforces the behaviors and attitudes that align with company values and drives performance. However, recognizing individuals effectively requires understanding their preferences, as not all employees appreciate recognition in the same way. Some thrive on public praise, while others may find it uncomfortable. A tailored approach, where recognition is aligned with an employee's preferences, is key to making them feel truly valued.

Knowing how each team member likes to be recognized so you can adapt your approach is crucial. *The 5 Languages of Appreciation in the Workplace* by Dr. Gary Chapman and Dr. Paul White offers an excellent framework for understanding these preferences.[47] The book includes an assessment tool that can spark meaningful conversations with employees about how they want to be recognized and appreciated. By incorporating this tool, leaders can ensure their recognition efforts are more personalized, leading to a deeper sense of value and connection.

Another powerful form of recognition is development. Recognizing that an employee's growth is just as important as their current achievements sends a message that you care about their future. Regularly asking employees questions like, "What keeps you excited about your work?", "What energizes you?" or "What would make you want to stay here long term?"—commonly referred to as stay interviews—provides invaluable insight into what drives them. Unlike exit interviews, which many companies rely on for feedback, stay interviews focus on the current relationship and what you can do now to foster engagement and retain high performers.

As a former HR executive, I can say that most people aren't truthful in exit interviews because they don't want to burn bridges. Stay interviews, however, allow leaders to understand what's truly important to employees, and ensure they are growing, learning, and feeling challenged in ways that align with their personal and professional goals.

ACTIONABLE STRATEGIES FOR APPRECIATION AND RECOGNITION

1. **Personalized Recognition**: Use tools like *The 5 Languages of Appreciation* to understand how employees like to be recognized, whether through public praise, written notes, acts of service, or other forms of appreciation.

2. **Tailor Your Approach**: Some employees enjoy public recognition, while others prefer private praise. Be mindful of these differences and adapt your approach to what feels most meaningful to each person.

3. **Stay Interviews**: Regularly ask employees what is most important to them, what keeps them engaged, and what would make them want to stay at the company. This not only shows that you value their input but also creates opportunities for professional development.

4. **Development as Recognition**: Support employees in their growth by providing opportunities for learning, mentoring, and skill-building. This can be a highly appreciated form of recognition that signals long-term investment in their success.

By recognizing and appreciating employees in a way that aligns with their preferences and needs, and by incorporating development into your recognition practices, you can create an environment where employees feel truly valued, engaged, and motivated to contribute their best work.

Managing Performance

A key responsibility of a leader is managing employee performance by setting clear expectations, providing coaching, delivering timely and meaningful feedback, and facilitating tough conversations when needed.

Traditionally, managers provided feedback only during annual reviews, leaving employees uncertain about their progress. Today's employees want ongoing clarity on where they stand, how they can improve, and what options exist for their career path. They expect regular conversations that help them grow and work toward their professional goals.

When an employee isn't meeting expectations, many managers default to a traditional "disciplinary action" approach. While documentation is important, a more effective strategy focuses on productive conversations that facilitate improvement. Most employees want to succeed, but they need ongoing feedback to adjust and improve. Feedback should help employees enhance their performance or reinforce what they are doing well.

Performance management is a continuous process, not a one-time event. Managers need to be intentional about having regular discussions around development opportunities. Mini, meaningful conversations throughout the year—whether about performance, career growth, or recognition—ensure employees stay engaged, supported, and clear on their path forward. The formal evaluation should simply document what has already been discussed, eliminating surprises and reinforcing a culture of growth.

> PERFORMANCE MANAGEMENT IS A CONTINUOUS PROCESS, NOT A ONE-TIME EVENT.

FEEDBACK THAT FUELS GROWTH

During my first week on the job at an IT company, a coworker made an offhand comment that stuck with me: "If our boss doesn't talk to you, that's usually a good sign." It reflected the traditional leadership style of the time: managers only engaged when there was a problem. Feedback was treated as a formal event, often limited to an annual review, rather than an ongoing conversation. But in today's workplace, effective feedback must be fluid, consistent, and integrated into regular coaching.

One of the main reasons employees leave organizations is a lack of feedback that supports their growth. Many managers struggle with this, often due to time constraints, discomfort, or not recognizing its impact. Yet, if your manager had information that could help you improve, wouldn't you want to know? Of course you would. So do your employees. They want clarity on their strengths, areas for improvement, and career growth opportunities.

When feedback is consistent and integrated into daily conversations, it becomes a natural part of the workplace rather than something saved for formal meetings. The best feedback is timely and continuous, reinforcing progress and addressing challenges before they become bigger issues.

Timely, constructive feedback empowers employees to perform at their best, strengthens relationships, and fosters an environment of trust and collaboration. Without it, performance stagnates, and opportunities for growth are missed. Unfortunately, many managers rely on vague praise like "You're doing a great job!" which, while positive, offers no specific guidance.

The first step in improving feedback is a mindset shift. Rather than seeing it as uncomfortable, leaders should view feedback as a tool for success that provides employees with the insights they need to grow and excel. Providing ongoing feedback is not just a leadership skill; it is essential for building a modern, engaged workplace.

IMPORTANT ELEMENTS FOR PROVIDING CONSTRUCTIVE FEEDBACK

- **Make feedback a regular part of coaching.** Consistently incorporating feedback into one-on-one meetings helps normalize it, reducing any stigma and making it a natural part of the development process.

- **Balance positive and constructive feedback.** Recognizing hard work and achievements reinforces strong performance, while constructive feedback provides clear guidance for improvement.

- **Focus on actions, not character.** Avoid using absolutes like "always" or "never," which can feel like personal attacks. Instead, reference specific behaviors, such as "I've noticed you've been late five times this month," to keep the conversation objective and performance-focused.

- **Be specific and provide examples.** Vague praise like "Great job!" is nice but not actionable. Instead, highlight the employee's specific actions and their impact, so they know what to continue or improve.

> • **Ditch the feedback sandwich.** Layering criticism between compliments can dilute the message and create confusion. Instead, be clear, direct, and supportive, ensuring feedback is constructive and meaningful.

Here are examples of effective feedback statements. Keep your feedback conversational, ensuring it feels authentic, respectful, and specific while maintaining a natural and approachable tone.

POSITIVE FEEDBACK EXAMPLES

- The way you handled the conflict with your coworker was very professional. I appreciate that you feel empowered to take ownership and address these issues on your own.
- I appreciate the way you took ownership of and fixed the issue with the report. Please continue to be as proactive as you have been about your work.
- Lisa, I can't thank you enough for your help with taxes this year. You handled the questionnaire, uploaded all the documents, and coordinated with our accountant, which saved me hours and made the process so much smoother.
- The way you handled that customer complaint was excellent. You listened and asked great questions, and when the customer got upset, you kept a patient and calm tone.

CONSTRUCTIVE FEEDBACK EXAMPLES

- I've noticed in the past three board reports that you made calculation mistakes that had an impact on what we presented. What ideas do you have for managing this going forward?
- I've noticed that you frequently interrupt team members during meetings. This is creating a stressful environment for your colleagues and keeping them from speaking up.

- I've noticed that in the last three meetings, you were frequently checking your phone. It is distracting to others and gives the impression that you aren't engaged.

A helpful way to provide clear and balanced feedback is using the framework: "It's okay to ___, but it's not okay to ___." For example, "It's okay to feel frustrated by the new policy, but it's not okay to complain about it to your employees." This approach acknowledges the individual's feelings while setting clear boundaries on acceptable behavior. I love using this framework in my parenting as well. For example, "It's okay to be mad at your sister, but it's not okay to hit her." (I've said variations of this sentence more times than I ever thought I would! ☺)

Feedback should not only address past actions but also be future-focused, guiding employees to make better choices and achieve improved performance. By framing feedback around what can be done differently moving forward, leaders create a path for growth rather than just pointing out mistakes. Ultimately, feedback is the foundation of effective coaching, helping employees develop, adapt, and succeed.

ELEVATING PERFORMANCE: THE POWER OF EMPLOYEE COACHING

Leadership used to be defined by authority—giving orders, solving problems, and making sure people followed directions. Like many new managers, I stepped into leadership without any formal training and little understanding of what effective leadership truly required. I spent most of my time managing tasks, making sure policies were followed, and stepping in to fix problems when they came up. My focus was on keeping things moving, putting out fires, and ensuring everyone stuck to the process. I was promoted because I was a strong individual contributor, but I hadn't yet developed the higher-level skills that actually make leaders effective—skills like influencing, coaching, and creating alignment.

It wasn't until I took an HR course that I started learning there was a better way. I began to understand how to delegate with clarity, create alignment around goals, and involve employees in decisions. But the biggest shift came a few years later when I enrolled in a coaching certification program. That experience transformed how I approached leadership.

I learned how to handle tough conversations and performance issues by being curious instead of critical. I started asking questions, getting to the root of the issue, and helping employees take ownership. And I learned how to do that with empathy and connection, not just structure and accountability.

I shifted from trying to manage every detail to focusing on trust, collaboration, and coaching my team to higher levels of effectiveness.

This shift in my own leadership reflects a broader evolution. For years, transactional leadership—focused on directing, telling, and fixing—was the norm. Those relational and developmental aspects of leadership simply weren't prioritized the way they are today. Today's workplace demands more—coaching, development, and human connection are no longer optional; they're essential to attracting and keeping top performers.

Modern leaders are expected to guide, mentor, and support employee growth. That means understanding individual needs, giving regular feedback, and fostering an environment where people can succeed. While this coaching-focused leadership takes more time and intention, it is essential for building strong teams and creating a healthy culture.

The best leaders make coaching an intentional daily practice, not just an occasional effort. Many managers mistake task discussions for coaching, but true coaching is about guiding employees to take ownership, work through challenges, and develop their full potential. Regular, meaningful conversations—beyond annual reviews—keep employees engaged and facilitate exceptional performance.

Coaching benefits both high performers and those who need support, and it doesn't have to be formal. Spontaneous coaching moments allow leaders to reinforce growth in real time. The most significant change in coaching is that leaders are transitioning from a mindset of fixing problems to one of facilitating growth and development.

To lead effectively in today's environment, leaders must shift from being fixers to being facilitators.

Fixing keeps you at the center of every problem, while facilitating empowers others to think critically, take ownership, and develop their skills. When you step back from being the sole problem-solver and instead guide your team through challenges, they develop enhanced skills, confidence, and accountability. This shift is not just about doing less; it's about leading in a way that develops stronger, more capable teams.

> TO LEAD EFFECTIVELY IN TODAY'S ENVIRONMENT, LEADERS MUST SHIFT FROM BEING FIXERS TO BEING FACILITATORS.

I want to highlight the importance of this shift. If there's one main theme you take away from this book, shifting your approach from fixing and doing to facilitating results through others can completely transform your leadership effectiveness.

The key to coaching and facilitating is curiosity—asking thoughtful questions to encourage growth and strengthen employees' critical thinking skills. For example, let's imagine an employee comes to their manager with a problem. The employee tells the manager that she is having a challenge getting information from a coworker in a different department, so she can't complete her project on time. Let's see how a manager using the traditional leadership approach (fixing) might handle this situation compared to the coaching approach.

TRADITIONAL APPROACH (FIXING)

The manager will likely respond in one of two ways.

- Tell the employee exactly how to handle this issue.
- Take the problem from the employee and handle it herself. In this case, go to the manager of the other employee to deal with the issue.

Coaching Approach (Facilitating)

Instead of taking ownership of the problem or allowing the employee to delegate it upward, the manager sees this as an opportunity to develop the employee's problem-solving skills. By coaching them through the situation, the manager encourages independent thinking and growth. Rather than providing immediate answers, they guide the employee with thoughtful questions to facilitate a solution.

- What do you think?
- How might you approach your coworker?

This approach may lead to a longer conversation as the manager helps the employee think through the best way to handle the situation. Instead of immediately stepping in, the manager encourages problem-solving by brainstorming solutions with the employee while guiding them toward taking ownership of the issue. The goal is to empower employees to handle challenges independently whenever possible, fostering accountability and preventing the manager from getting unnecessarily involved in tasks that can be resolved more efficiently without their direct intervention.

Of course, there are times when managerial involvement is necessary. However, in most cases, employees can be developed to handle tasks, issues, and problems on their own. One of the biggest drains on a manager's time is stepping into low-level issues that the team should handle.

This shift can be challenging because many managers are conditioned to step in and fix problems. But if day-to-day issues constantly consume you, you'll struggle to find time for the bigger, more impactful work of caretaking the culture.

Cultivating Curiosity Through Questions

Curiosity is a vital leadership skill that strengthens your impact and enhances your ability to navigate difficult conversations. Thoughtful questions open the lines of communication, fostering engagement and deeper dialogue. When used effectively, questions create meaningful conversations, not just with employees, but also with your manager, colleagues, significant other, and even your children.

Questions serve many purposes, from professional development and performance management to problem solving and conflict resolution.

TIPS FOR USING QUESTIONS EFFECTIVELY

- Ask open-ended questions that encourage employees to elaborate.
- Resist the urge to provide immediate answers; coach employees to think through solutions.
- Avoid "Why" questions, as they can feel accusatory. Instead, use "How" or "What" to keep conversations productive.

EXAMPLES OF IMPACTFUL QUESTIONS

TO START A CONVERSATION

- *What's on your mind?*
- *What is the most important thing we should be discussing today?*[48]
- *What is your biggest challenge right now?*
- *What would be the best use of our time today?*

FOR PROFESSIONAL DEVELOPMENT

- *What skills do you want to develop in the next year?*
- *What kind of work excites and challenges you the most?*
- *What strengths do you want to leverage more in your work?*
- *Are there any projects or responsibilities you'd like to take on to expand your experience?*
- *What does career success look like for you?*

- *What support or resources would help you achieve your professional goals?*
- *If you could design your ideal role, what would it include?*
- *What's one area where you'd like to improve, and how can I support you in that?*

For Understanding Situations

- *What happened?*
- *What have you learned from this?*
- *How might you handle a similar situation differently next time?*
- *How could you approach your coworker to resolve this issue?*
- *What are your ideas for solving this problem?*
- *What do you think?*

To Challenge Employees

- *What does the data tell you?*
- *What alternative solutions have you considered?*
- *What's your next step?*
- *How might you approach this issue?*

By leading with curiosity and asking the right questions, you empower employees to think critically, take ownership, and develop their problem-solving skills while strengthening trust and communication.

Addressing Performance Challenges

One of the biggest contributors to low team engagement is conflict avoidance and passive leadership—hallmarks of the *leadership saboteurs*. Avoiding issues doesn't make them go away; it allows them to fester and build, creating frustration among high-performing employees and making the problem harder to address.

One key to addressing performance issues is to have the conversation as soon as you notice a pattern. This early window is a valuable opportunity because it allows you to address the concern in a more casual, supportive way before it grows into a bigger problem. This proactive approach also significantly reduces discomfort and prevents the issue from escalating. When managers delay and let issues fester, the situation often becomes bigger and more uncomfortable, leading to further avoidance.

When an employee falls short of expectations, use a coaching approach rather than defaulting to reprimands. A traditional "disciplinary action" mindset is often reactive, blame-focused, and past-oriented, making employees more likely to become defensive or disengaged.

A coaching approach, grounded in curiosity, fosters accountability and engagement. Instead of dwelling on past mistakes, the manager shares observations and shifts the focus to the future by asking thoughtful questions. Employees are more likely to participate in the conversation and offer solutions when the focus is on what they can do moving forward—what they can control—rather than on past behavior, which they cannot change. This does not mean ignoring past issues; instead, it means using coaching questions to acknowledge the situation while guiding the discussion toward solutions. Shifting the focus to the future creates a sense of responsibility and ownership, leading to real growth and improved performance, rather than blame and defensiveness.

Two of my go-to coaching phrases are *"I've noticed"* and *"I'm sensing."*

These neutral, non-confrontational openers help initiate conversations without triggering defensiveness.

For example, let's say an employee has been consistently late to work for the past month. Here's an example of how you can facilitate this conversation.

"Amy, the reason I want to meet today is because *I've noticed* you have been late five times over the past few weeks."

- Follow up the statement with a question.

"What's going on?" or "What's happening?" or "What is contributing to this issue?"

- Listen to what the employee says. This is important. You want this to be a dialogue, not a lecture. You are not responsible for fixing it.
- Paraphrase and follow up with a question to elicit ownership.

"It sounds like you have been having issues with your transportation. (You might have a short, natural conversation about this challenge.) Then you ask a question to elicit ownership.

"What can you do to make sure you are here on time each day?" (Shifting ownership to the employee and having them come up with the solution.)

Sometimes it's helpful to set a follow-up meeting to check in on progress. This is a way to instill accountability and ensure resolution.

But what if the employee doesn't improve?

In that case, continue with the coaching approach, but gradually intensify your language and approach. Think of it like turning up a dial—becoming more direct and firmer with each conversation, while still maintaining respect.

For example, if the employee you addressed about lateness hasn't shown improvement, it's time to take a firmer stance.

This is how you might handle a follow-up meeting.

"Amy, we had a conversation a couple of weeks ago about your pattern of being late to work. During that conversation, you said you would ensure you were getting to work on time. I've noticed that you have still been late over the past two weeks. What's going on?"

{Allow Amy to respond}

"Unfortunately, I do need to formally document our conversation this time. Your lateness is impacting the team, and your coworkers are having to take on some of the workload while you are not here. What can you do to ensure you are here on time starting tomorrow?"

If the situation still doesn't improve, you meet with Amy again and take an even firmer stance. It might sound like this:

"Amy, we've met three times about your pattern of lateness, and there has been no improvement. I'm perplexed because when we meet, you say you will make an effort to be on time, but things haven't changed. What's getting in the way of you being here on time?"

{Allow Amy to respond}

"I need you to know that if there is not a significant improvement this week, we will be moving to terminate your employment."

If the employee becomes defensive, focus on responding thoughtfully, rather than impulsively. Take a moment to pause, collect your thoughts, and manage your emotions before continuing the conversation.

Maintain respect and clarity with the employee about next steps, while actively engaging them in the conversation by asking questions to foster dialogue. If you're dealing with an employee who is not performing, it's always advisable to involve your human resources department. These situations can be complex, so it's crucial to follow company procedures and collaborate with an HR professional who not only understands the nuances of your specific case but is also knowledgeable about the employment laws in your state.

In a more traditional work environment, managers often default to "write-ups" and disciplinary action as the primary response to performance issues. While documentation and adherence to company policy are still important, I believe they can be balanced with a coaching approach—one that engages the employee in the discussion, clarifies expectations, and instills accountability. This combination allows you to address the issue respectfully while still achieving effective results.

When navigating challenging conversations or performance issues, here are some open-ended questions that can be particularly helpful.

- What happened?
- What led to this situation?
- What obstacles did you encounter?
- How has this impacted the team?
- How will you approach this differently in the future?

- What support do you need from me?
- What insights have you gained from this experience?
- What have you learned from this situation?

After the conversation, be sure to document what was discussed. Even if it was just a verbal exchange, proper documentation is essential. Additionally, make sure to follow up and follow through.

If you observe a decline in performance again, address it promptly as soon as you notice the issue persisting. And, of course, if you see improvements, be sure to acknowledge and praise the employee for their progress.

One approach I've found helpful in facilitating challenging conversations, whether with an employee, a colleague, or even a family member, is to be "invested yet detached." This means you are fully committed to the conversation, to how you show up, and to your role in it, but you remain detached from the outcome. You can control your response, but you can't control how the other person will react. It's important not to judge the success of the conversation solely by their reaction. For example, if an employee becomes defensive, you can focus on how you respond, using your influence to guide the discussion.

There have been times when I've tried coaching, giving feedback, and guiding an employee, but despite my best efforts, things haven't been successful. I can't change that. What I can do is be *invested* in the process, but *detached* from the result. While your approach can significantly influence the outcome, there will be occasions when your efforts don't lead to the desired result.

As a leader, you want to feel good knowing that you approached the situation thoughtfully, followed the right steps, and did your part to create a better outcome. If things don't work out, at least you can feel good about how you approached the situation.

When I was leading HR at the credit union, one of my managers was responsible for creating a training workshop for our management team. Each week during our one-on-ones, she assured me she was making progress, but something in her tone and energy made me question that. I made the mistake of letting it go and not pressing further until six weeks later, when the CEO asked me for an update, and I realized I needed to dig deeper. In my next meeting with her, I used the "I'm sensing" approach.

I said, "I'm sensing that you might be having some challenges with this project. Is that right?" She became emotional and admitted she felt completely overwhelmed and hadn't made much progress. As a leader, I'd always rather know there's a challenge so we can work through it, rather than leave it unspoken. The real mistake I made was not surfacing this conversation earlier, when I first sensed something was off. We could have avoided weeks of stalled progress if I had followed my intuition. But once she acknowledged she was struggling, it gave us a chance to move forward.

I was tempted to take the project on myself or tell her exactly what to do, but I recognized this as a valuable opportunity to build her skills. I asked if it would be helpful to spend the next hour out-lining the project together, and she said yes. I guided her by asking, "If you were to break this project into three phases, what would they be?" From there, we built it step by step. I shared occasional insights, but the focus stayed on her thinking and solutions. By the end of the hour, she had a clear direction, renewed confidence, and we set up weekly check-ins to maintain momentum. She ultimately completed the project successfully. That experience taught me a lasting lesson: when you sense something is off, don't wait—lean into the conversation.

COACHING AND DELEGATING FOR GROWTH

One of the most valuable ways to use coaching as a leader is to help employees take responsibility for their decisions. While some decisions require leadership involvement, many employees default to seeking approval or guidance for situations they should be handling independently.

When employees push decisions back to their managers unnecessarily, it's known as upward delegation. Whether intentional or not, they are shifting ownership of the problem to you. This can happen for several reasons: a lack of confidence, fear of making a mistake, or simply being accustomed to having a manager step in.

As a leader, your role isn't to be the sole decision-maker; it's to empower your team to think critically, problem-solve, and develop their skills. Delegating decision-making enables you to concentrate on high-impact priorities and maintain a strategic focus while also empowering your employees by giving them valuable opportunities to develop their skills, build confidence, and grow professionally.

This process takes time, and mistakes may happen. The key is to support employees in their learning, so they become more capable, independent, and effective, ultimately benefiting both them and you.

If you find employees frequently trying to delegate upward, use coaching questions to redirect ownership back to them.

- What do you think?
- What solutions have you considered?
- How would you handle this if I weren't here?
- What options do you have?
- How will you gain buy-in from the team?
- What's your next step?

If an employee responds with "I don't know," encourage them to brainstorm. Offer one idea and ask, "What's another approach you can think of?" This helps them develop problem-solving skills rather than relying on you for answers.

By fostering independent decision-making, you build a stronger, more capable team while keeping yourself focused on the bigger picture.

MEANINGFUL ONE-ON-ONE MEETINGS

Most managers treat one-on-ones as status checks. While progress tracking matters, these meetings are far more valuable when the focus shifts from task updates to coaching and delegation. Instead of spending precious minutes reviewing every detail, use a shared document to record tasks, goals, and progress between meetings. Then, reserve your one-on-one time for removing roadblocks, coaching through challenges, and handing off new responsibilities.

In my own team meetings, we often intentionally create time for me to either train a team member, delegate a project, or discuss strategic goals. This not only frees me up to work in my Key Result Areas, but it also helps develop employees by giving them opportunities to take ownership and contribute in new ways.

The time you spend in one-on-ones is valuable for creating clarity, building trust, and empowering employees to take ownership of their work. By being more intentional with these meetings, you can develop your team while keeping your focus on strategic priorities.

STRATEGIES FOR MORE MEANINGFUL ONE-ON-ONE CONVERSATIONS

1. **Start the Meeting with Intention**

   Begin with open-ended questions that invite reflection and discussion.

   - *What's on your mind?*
   - *What is the biggest challenge you are facing right now?*
   - *What is most important for us to focus on today?*

2. **Assess What's Working and What's Not**

   Encourage employees to evaluate their experiences and identify areas for improvement.

   - *What's going well for you right now?*
   - *What's not working as well as you'd like?*
   - *What's one thing I can do to better support you?*

3. **Encourage Employees to Come Prepared**

   One-on-one meetings should be interactive conversations, not just a manager-led check-in. To make them more meaningful and productive, set the expectation that employees come prepared. Encourage them to reflect in advance on the areas that matter most to their progress and development. You can provide a few guiding questions to help them think through what they want to discuss:

- *What do I need help with? What's my biggest challenge?*
- *What are my top two accomplishments from the past week?*
- *What are my top two priorities for this week?*
- *Where do I need support?*
- *Is anything blocking progress toward my goals?*

When employees take time to reflect before the meeting, the conversation becomes more focused, collaborative, and impactful.

4. **Coach Through a Challenge**

   When an employee is facing an obstacle, guide them through it rather than providing immediate answers.

   - *Would it be helpful to use the next half hour to map out an approach?*
   - *If you broke this project into three phases, what would they be?*
   - *What's the first step you can take?*

5. **Ending with a Clear Recap**

   Wrap up by reinforcing key takeaways and next steps to ensure alignment and accountability.

   - *What are your biggest takeaways from this meeting?*
   - *What are your next steps, and when will you complete them?*
   - *What are your top three priorities for this week?*

By structuring your one-on-ones with a focus on **coaching, problem-solving,** and **strategic discussions**, you create more valuable conversations that facilitate both employee development and business impact.

IMPACTFUL TEAM MEETINGS

Just like your one-on-one meetings, your team meetings should be intentional, effective, and engaging. The key is to maximize this valuable time by focusing on what truly matters. Instead of simply running through updates, take 10 minutes beforehand to clarify the meeting's purpose and priorities.

Ask yourself:

- *What are the two most important things I need to share with my team right now?*
- *What goals or initiatives are we working toward, and what progress have we made?*
- *Why does this goal or initiative matter? What impact will it have on the team and the organization?*

CONNECT THE TEAM TO THE "WHY"

One of the most effective ways to gain buy-in and motivate your team is to clearly connect their work to a larger purpose. When people understand *why* something matters, not just *what* needs to be done, they're more likely to feel engaged, take ownership, and contribute with intention.

Whether it's a new initiative, a shift in process, or a performance goal, take the time to explain the reasoning behind it. Share the bigger picture, including both the business impact and the benefit to the team. This builds trust, strengthens commitment, and invites collaboration.

For example:

"Over the next six months, we're focusing on reducing waste. Currently, our waste level stands at 13 percent, resulting in annual costs of over $130,000 for materials and an additional $120,000 in lost productivity. Our goal is to reduce waste by at least 5 percent this quarter, which would save over $84,000. Beyond the financial impact, cutting waste will reduce rework, saving time and frustration for everyone. Let's take a few minutes to discuss ideas. What suggestions do you have?"

This kind of transparent, inclusive communication transforms a directive into a shared mission, and it's one of the simplest, most powerful ways to elevate performance and culture.

LEVERAGE MEETINGS FOR CLARITY AND COLLABORATION

Use your team meetings as a platform to:

- Create clarity around priorities and expectations.
- Work through challenges and roadblocks.
- Communicate the "why" behind decisions and initiatives.
- Encourage ownership by involving employees in brainstorming and problem-solving.

By shifting team meetings from routine updates to meaningful discussions, you foster engagement, alignment, and shared accountability, making each meeting a productive and valuable experience. We'll explore more about how to facilitate effective meetings in Chapter 13.

* * *

In today's world, effective leadership requires a relational approach—one that prioritizes connection, coaching, feedback, and employee development. As a leader, you must be empathetic, adaptable, authentic, and an excellent communicator. These qualities are essential in building trust, fostering engagement, and inspiring loyalty among your team. Being true to yourself and your values enables you to create a strong foundation of trust that creates both individual and organizational success.

Additionally, employee development is key to a thriving culture. By providing opportunities for continuous learning and embracing new challenges, leaders empower their teams to grow, adapt, and innovate. Investing in employee growth not only strengthens individual performance but also cultivates a culture of ongoing improvement.

But caretaking the culture goes beyond the positive elements like appreciation, recognition, and coaching. It also involves caretaking your team as a system, ensuring that all parts of the team are functioning at their best. As a leader, it's your responsibility to address challenges and issues promptly and effectively, so they don't drag down team morale or engagement. Active leadership means staying attuned to both the successes and the struggles within your team and responding proactively to maintain a healthy and productive environment.

As you move forward in your leadership journey, remember that caretaking the culture is not just about managing tasks; it's about shaping an environment where your team feels valued, engaged, and motivated to succeed. This leads to more fulfilling work experiences and better business outcomes.

13

FACILITATE RESULTS

You can't build a reputation on what you are going to do.

—Henry Ford

In many organizations, accountability is viewed negatively, often seen as blame rather than responsibility. This causes people to avoid ownership out of fear of being reprimanded. Traditional management reinforced this mindset, with leaders acting as fixers and enforcers, relying on oversight and correction to drive results. While this approach may have worked in the short term, it often left managers chasing people down to ensure tasks were completed, and created organizations where employees simply did the work without real engagement or connection to it.

True accountability isn't about blame; it's about responsibility.

Modern leadership takes a different approach. Instead of solving every problem and enforcing accountability after the fact, effective leaders create the conditions for accountability in advance—by setting clear expectations, building strong structures, and fostering a culture that supports follow-through. While occasional course corrections are still necessary, these strategies greatly reduce the need for them.

As leaders, our goal is not to hold people accountable in a punitive way, but to *instill* accountability by creating a culture where individuals take ownership of their actions and outcomes. Accountability, at its core, is about personal responsibility and following through.

Roger Conners and Tom Smith define accountability as "A personal choice to rise above one's circumstances and demonstrate the ownership necessary for achieving desired results—to see it, own it, solve it, and do it."[49]

Accountability is not just a process; it's a mindset. It's one of the most powerful traits behind both personal and professional success. And it always starts with you.

When our oldest daughter, Olivia, was seven, my husband Rino and I found ourselves deep in a late-night conversation about parenting and the kind of adults we hoped our children would eventually become. We spoke about the values we wanted to instill, like kindness, generosity, confidence, and responsibility. Then we shifted to habits. What small, daily actions could help build those values over time?

Rino suggested we have Olivia start making her bed each morning. He felt that it was a simple habit that set a positive tone for the day. More importantly, it teaches her to take pride in her space and be responsible for her environment. I agreed with his point, but after a brief pause, I asked, "Don't you think we should start making our bed first?"

After that conversation, Rino and I made our bed every single morning. We did it consistently for six months before ever bringing it up with Olivia. When we finally introduced the expectation to her, it was not just a rule; it was a reflection of what she had already seen modeled every day.

That moment stuck with me. It was a powerful reminder that accountability starts with us. Whether at home or in the workplace, the best way to inspire ownership in others is to demonstrate it ourselves. Our actions speak louder than our words ever could.

Your team is always observing and drawing cues from your behavior. If you want them to take ownership, you have to model it consistently through your own actions. Leaders often focus on how to make others more accountable, without realizing that they may be falling short in setting a good example. When you don't follow through on your commitments, show up inconsistently, or fail to communicate clearly, it slowly erodes trust and engagement.

Often, the breakdown isn't in the big things. It's in the small moments—the missed opportunities, the unspoken words, or the unchecked behaviors. These actions may not be intentional, but they have an impact. For example, a manager may neglect to provide important feedback because they are too busy. While there's no ill intent, the effect is still a missed opportunity to coach and build trust. And by failing to deliver on this key leadership responsibility, the manager is not modeling accountability.

Your leadership behaviors have a direct impact on team results. Whether positive or negative, your actions shape your team's performance and its culture. The small things matter. Over time, they either build trust and alignment or slowly chip away at integrity and connection.

HOW LEADERS CAN UNINTENTIONALLY FAIL TO MODEL ACCOUNTABILITY

- Being consistently late to meetings
- Neglecting to give important feedback
- Canceling or frequently rescheduling meetings
- Responding to an email when angry
- Neglecting to show appreciation for great work
- Missing the chance to regularly connect with and invest in your top performers
- Complaining about an employee (instead of talking with them)
- Not being prepared for meetings
- Not answering emails in a timely manner
- Not following through with what you said you would do

Even the smallest behaviors send signals. They shape your team's perception of your leadership and set the tone for how they show up every day.

Ask yourself: *What are three ways I can increase ownership and accountability and model it for my team?*

Leadership isn't about control—it's about consistency. It's about showing up in the everyday moments with clarity, intention, and integrity. When you lead with that kind of ownership, you set the tone, and your team is far more likely to follow your example and take ownership themselves.

FROM CONTROL TO COMMITMENT: BUILDING A CULTURE OF OWNERSHIP AND RESULTS

The ability to facilitate results is a critical aspect of leadership success. Every organization exists to achieve outcomes, but how a leader facilitates that process makes all the difference. Traditional leadership often relies on authority, directives, and, when issues arise, disciplinary action to enforce accountability. In contrast, exceptional leaders take a more strategic approach— establishing clear expectations, creating structures that support follow-through, and fostering a culture of accountability built on respect and clarity rather than command and control.

To facilitate accountability and high performance, leaders must create the conditions that support it from the start. This means shifting from constantly fixing problems to facilitating success by designing systems and setting expectations that make follow-through part of how work gets done. While there will still be times when missed commitments need to be addressed, these strategies significantly reduce how often those conversations are necessary.

You can invest deeply in building a positive team culture, fostering camaraderie, and creating an environment where people enjoy coming to work, but if your team is not achieving meaningful results, then you are not an effective leader. Teams need both strong teamwork *and* results to thrive. Some managers focus so much on creating a positive environment that they fail to guide their teams toward consistent performance. Others take a more traditional approach, driving hard for results but neglecting the health and engagement of the team. Exceptional leaders strike the right balance—they create clarity, nurture a healthy culture, and empower others to deliver outstanding results.

YOUR LANGUAGE IMPACTS YOUR RESULTS

In *Winning with Accountability*, Henry Evans introduces the concept of the "Language of Failure"—vague phrases like "ASAP," "I'll try," or "someone should," that create ambiguity, erode trust, and undermine results.[50] These phrases leave room for interpretation and limit true ownership, often leading to missed deadlines, confusion, and finger-pointing. Exceptional results require clear, specific, and actionable language. When leaders and teams commit to clearly defining who will do what, and by when, accountability strengthens, and follow-through improves. Clear language isn't just a communication tactic; it's a performance driver. By eliminating the Language of Failure and replacing it with precise commitments, leaders set the stage for clarity, alignment, and consistent execution.

The glossary of failure consists of vague and weak words or phrases, causing a breakdown of ownership and poor results.

- Soon
- ASAP
- Right Away
- I'll get on it
- Later
- Try
- Should
- I'll do my best
- When you get a chance…
- By the next time we meet…

One phrase I've had to work on in my own leadership is, "When you get a chance." It sounds polite and flexible, but it often creates confusion and delays. I once asked a team member on a Monday,

"When you get a chance, can you mail this package for me?" She said yes, and I assumed it would go out that day. But several days later, the recipient followed up, asking if I had sent it because they hadn't received the package. I checked in with my team member, and she said she had mailed it *that morning*, which was Thursday. I hadn't been clear, and this misunderstanding was entirely my responsibility. I left it open to interpretation when I really meant, "Are you able to mail this today?" In my effort to be nice and approachable, I used vague language that did not help me get the task done and also did not provide the clarity my employee needed. It ended up creating confusion instead of support.

So often, we soften our language to avoid sounding demanding or bossy. We want to be kind and approachable—but in doing so, we risk being vague. The truth is, you can be both clear and respectful. In fact, employees *want* clarity. They appreciate knowing what you need and when you need it. It's not micromanaging; it's effective leadership.

Be specific in your communication.

- This report needs to be presented to the Board of Directors on Friday at 12:00. Are you able to submit the report to me by Thursday at 5:00 so I have time to review it?
- Please submit your report by Tuesday at 5:00.
- Are you able to make these corrections by 12:00 today?

All of these phrases are both clear and respectful.

Clarity is one of the simplest yet most powerful tools for facilitating better results. You can be both respectful and clear, and your team will appreciate knowing exactly what is expected of them. Start by noticing when you use vague language and set the intention to be more direct and specific. I also suggest bringing this up in a team meeting so your team members can focus on being more specific. Let your team know that you've observed that, while everyone is kind and collaborative, the language used is often too vague, and you'd like to work together to create a culture where clarity is the norm by eliminating language like "ASAP" and "soon". Even small shifts in how you communicate can lead to stronger follow-through, less confusion, and better performance.

ENCOURAGE YOUR TEAM TO ASK FOR CLARITY

Creating a culture of clarity doesn't stop with how you communicate; it also involves encouraging your team to speak up and ask for clarity when they need it. Make this a standard practice on your team. Let them know that questions are not a sign of weakness, but a sign of ownership and accountability. And model it yourself. When you are unclear about your role, responsibilities, a deadline, or next steps, demonstrate leadership by asking for clarity from your manager or peers. This not only helps you be more effective, but it sets the tone for your team to do the same. Clarity at every level strengthens execution, reduces misunderstandings, and creates better results.

No matter what your level in the organization, asking for clarity demonstrates that you are taking ownership and want everyone to be successful.

To reinforce a culture of clarity, encourage your team to ask for the information they need, especially when you're delegating a task or project. Prompting your employees to seek clarity not only helps prevent misunderstandings but also builds their confidence in speaking up. Use language that encourages open dialogue and normalizes questions.

- What's not clear?
- What did I miss?
- What other information would be helpful?
- What questions do you have? (This is more effective than "Do you have any questions?" because it assumes there are questions and normalizes asking.)

These simple shifts in how you invite dialogue can make a big impact on clarity, ownership, and ultimately, results.

CONSISTENCY OVER CHAOS: COMMUNICATING IN A DISTRACTED WORLD

George Bernard Shaw once said, "The single biggest problem in communication is the illusion that it has taken place." In today's workplace, that illusion is amplified by constant digital noise. Employees are inundated with communications across various channels, leading to potential misunderstandings and decreased productivity. A study by Loom, Inc. revealed that the average worker spends approximately 3 hours and 43 minutes daily on emails, messaging, video, or phone calls.[51] This constant influx of information can result in messages being overlooked or misinterpreted. In addition, employees are also navigating an environment of shifting priorities, which makes focusing on the right things even more challenging.

As leaders, one of our most important responsibilities is to create clarity in a constantly changing environment. With endless distractions and priorities shifting quickly, saying something once is rarely enough. We must communicate consistently and clearly to ensure our messages are not only heard but truly understood. The challenge isn't overcommunicating; it's making sure key priorities are clear, remembered, and acted upon. By reinforcing important points and aligning our communication with what matters most, we help our teams stay focused, follow through, and perform at their best. Clear, deliberate communication is essential for cutting through the noise and leading effectively.

ACCOUNTABILITY STRUCTURES: FROM INTENT TO ACTION

One of the most effective ways to foster accountability is by embedding it into the way your team operates. When leaders are intentional about communication, check-ins, and workflows, they create an environment where ownership is built into the process, not something that has to be constantly chased or enforced. Clear structures serve as the foundation for follow-through, helping team members stay aligned, understand expectations, and take ownership of their work. These systems act as built-in reminders that reinforce priorities and encourage proactive behavior. When accountability is supported from the start through thoughtful, consistent practices, the need for reactive correction is significantly reduced.

ACCOUNTABILITY STRUCTURES THAT PROMOTE OWNERSHIP AND FOLLOW-THROUGH

- **Designated note-taker during team meetings:** Ensures key decisions, action items, and deadlines are clearly captured and not overlooked.

- **End-of-meeting recap of takeaways and responsibilities:** Reinforces clarity around who is doing what by when, minimizing confusion and dropped tasks.

- **Individual coaching sessions or one-on-one meetings:** Create space for ongoing support, progress check-ins, and accountability-focused conversations. These meetings not only strengthen communication and development but also ensure alignment and forward progress, serving as built-in checkpoints to keep priorities on track and goals moving forward.

- **Performance management processes or formal evaluations:** Provide structured opportunities to assess progress and set clear goals for the year.

- **Regular feedback:** Keeps expectations clear and enables timely course correction and continuous improvement.

- **Project or status check-ins:** Establish a consistent rhythm for reviewing progress and maintaining accountability.

- **Weekly status emails:** Offer a written snapshot of priorities and progress, helping everyone stay aligned and focused.

- **Weekly office hours:** Create an open, intentional space for questions, updates, or support, reinforcing a culture of ownership and accessibility.

Many managers unintentionally set their teams up for confusion and missed opportunities by failing to establish clear structures for clarity, follow-through, and check-ins. Without a specific process for setting expectations and revisiting progress, employees are often unclear from the start. With no built-in checkpoints, there's nothing in place to keep things on track. This lack of structure leads to lost time, decreased productivity, and unnecessary rework.

I'm often surprised, during the leadership programs I facilitate, by how many managers don't hold regular one-on-one meetings with their team members. When done well, these meetings are not just check-ins; they're invaluable conversations that provide clarity, offer support, drive momentum, and build alignment toward results. Used consistently, these simple yet powerful structures help weave accountability into the fabric of the team's culture and increase achievement, engagement, and a shared sense of ownership for both individual and team results.

When facilitating results, incorporating coaching questions can be a powerful way to create clarity, ignite ownership, and help employees move from intention to action. Rather than simply assigning tasks, asking thoughtful, open-ended questions encourages team members to reflect, prioritize, and take responsibility for their next steps. Questions like "What will you focus on this week?" or "What are your next two action steps?" promote alignment and help clarify expectations. This approach not only facilitates results but also empowers employees to think critically, stay accountable, and remain engaged in their work. In your coaching sessions, one-on-one meetings, and daily interactions, coaching questions can instill ownership and accountability.

EXAMPLES OF ACCOUNTABILITY QUESTIONS

- What is your biggest takeaway from our meeting?
- What will you focus on this week?
- What is not clear? What other details do you need?
- What are your next two action steps?

- Who is responsible for this action?
- How will you let me know this is completed?
- When will this be completed?
- Who do you need to involve to complete this project on time?
- What do you need to do to focus completely on this project today?
- What tasks can you delegate so you can free up your time?
- Based on what I just shared, what do you think are the top three takeaways?
- What needs to be done to ensure the project is a success?
- What other departments need to be involved in this process?
- What questions do you have?
- What are we missing?

If an employee does not follow through or meet expectations, you can use coaching questions to help them reflect, take ownership, and move toward accountability and improvement.

Questions When Employees Fall Short or Miss Expectations

- What happened?
- What have you learned from this situation?
- How might you handle this situation differently in the future?
- How might you approach your co-worker to resolve this issue?
- What are your ideas for fixing this problem?
- What do you think?

By establishing strong accountability structures and using coaching to support ownership, leaders can create a culture where follow-through becomes the norm. But what happens when an employee still doesn't meet expectations, even with support and clarity?

From Frustration to Follow-Through: Handling Unmet Expectations Effectively

Even with clear communication and strong accountability structures in place, there will be times when an employee doesn't follow through or meet expectations. These situations can feel frustrating, but they're also opportunities for meaningful conversations to get things back on track. Instead of defaulting to blame or avoidance, effective leaders approach missed expectations with curiosity, clarity, and a commitment to helping the employee course correct.

Traditionally, when an employee doesn't meet expectations, the default response was to "hold them accountable" through a disciplinary process that defaulted to formal write-ups. While documenting performance and following your organization's policies is important and necessary, it's equally important to recognize that these moments can be approached in a way that fosters responsibility and ownership rather than blame and reprimands. As we discussed in Chapter 12, curiosity and thoughtful questions are some of the most powerful tools a leader can use when addressing unmet expectations.

Holding someone accountable is not the same as placing blame on them. Blame focuses on what went wrong and who's at fault, often triggering defensiveness and disengagement. Responsibility, on the other hand, invites reflection and identifies what needs to happen next. It encourages learning, growth, and a stronger sense of ownership.

Effective leaders understand this distinction and resist the urge to dwell on the past. While it may be necessary to share examples of what has already occurred, the real power lies in shifting the conversation to what can be done moving forward. This future-focused approach helps employees take responsibility and builds a culture where accountability is not feared, but embraced as a path to improvement and success.

> - **Blame** is reactive, rooted in the past, and often driven by the ego. It focuses on making someone feel bad, guilty, or isolated; essentially, "teaching a lesson" through punishment. The natural human response to this approach is defensiveness, which doesn't lead to a productive result.
>
>   *Example: "Why are you late?"* (Past-focused and accusatory)
>
> - **Responsibility** is proactive, focused on the future, and grounded in action. It's about responding with intention and creating space for ownership and improvement. Responsibility doesn't ignore the issue; it addresses it in a way that promotes growth and accountability.
>
>   *Example: "I've noticed you've been late twice this week. What's going on? What will you do to make sure you're on time starting tomorrow?"* (Future-focused and solution-oriented)

You can absolutely document performance concerns and follow your company's guidelines while still using a coaching approach. For example, your initial conversation with an employee might be informal and supportive, aimed at understanding what's going on and clarifying expectations. You can document that discussion on the back end in your notes, even if it's not a formal write-up. If the behavior doesn't improve, you can continue to coach while also escalating the process according to your company's policies, including formal documentation, when necessary. The key is that you're still being clear about expectations, but you're doing it in a way that encourages the employee to take ownership and responsibility. This approach respects the required process while also promoting quicker and more lasting improvement because it's rooted in collaboration rather than consequences.

Through your conversations, if an employee is not taking ownership or accountability, it may be helpful to assess the underlying reasons before taking action. Begin by evaluating whether they have the necessary skills and knowledge to meet expectations. If there are gaps in training, providing additional support, resources, or mentoring may help. Beyond technical skills, consider other factors such as clarity of expectations, workload balance, and engagement level. Sometimes, employees struggle with accountability because they do not fully understand what is expected of them or feel overwhelmed by competing priorities.

Once skill and resource gaps are ruled out, focus on communication. Have a direct yet supportive conversation with the employee, using a coaching approach. Ask open-ended questions to understand their perspective and encourage self-reflection. Reinforce the importance of their role and the impact of their contributions. If issues persist, outline clear consequences while providing guidance on how they

> ACCOUNTABILITY IS ABOUT HANDLING TOUGH CONVERSATIONS IN A WAY THAT IS BOTH FIRM AND RESPECTFUL.

can improve. Consistency in addressing accountability issues ensures fairness across the organization and helps reinforce expectations.

If your coaching efforts are not producing results, it may be time to turn up the heat by being even more direct about your expectations and the possible consequences of continued issues. Accountability is about handling tough conversations in a way that is both firm and respectful. It means addressing them with clarity and respect. You can be both firm and fair by clearly outlining what needs to change, why it matters, and what will happen if expectations are not met. Directness does not have to be harsh; it's about removing ambiguity so that the employee fully understands their responsibilities. When leaders balance accountability with respect, they create an environment where employees know what is expected, feel supported in their growth, and understand that accountability is a standard, not an option.

When it comes to handling challenging conversations, there are two mantras I've developed that have helped me navigate challenging situations with greater calm and clarity.

Be with What Is: This reminds me to stay grounded in the reality of the moment, especially when things feel out of my control. As leaders and humans, we often waste energy resisting reality or replaying what we could have done differently. For example, when one of my kids gets a low grade on a test, it's easy to slip into self-blame or rumination. But that doesn't help anyone. Instead, I remind myself to be with what is—accept the moment for what it is and focus on what can be done now.

Be Invested, Yet Detached: I introduced this concept in the last chapter, and it's especially helpful when preparing for a challenging conversation. It means showing up with intention, care, and clarity without getting attached to a specific outcome. You can be fully invested in how you prepare, how you communicate, and how you support someone, but you can't control how they'll respond. Just like I can't take a test for my child, I can't force an employee to change. I can show up well, but the response is up to them.

These mindsets help shift our energy away from trying to control others and toward leading with presence, clarity, and emotional steadiness.

ASSESS YOUR CONTRIBUTION

We talked about the movie in your head in Chapter 11. As leaders, we are not always good about giving specifics or context that can be important for employees to take ownership and be accountable.

When people are clear, they become accountable. But when someone fails to meet expectations, instead of automatically assuming they misunderstood, ask yourself what part you played in the failure. Pause and reflect before jumping to conclusions.

- Did you provide clear instructions?
- Did you give a deadline?
- Did you make it clear that this was a priority?

Instilling accountability doesn't have to come with tension or negativity. When done with clarity, consistency, and respect, it creates a culture where follow-through is expected, ownership is embraced, and performance improves more naturally. By shifting from blame to responsibility and integrating simple structures that support follow-through, you can build trust while still focusing on results.

Passive and conflict-avoidant leaders often struggle with accountability because they default to a reactive or hands-off style, avoiding difficult conversations and failing to set clear expectations up front. This lack of structure makes it harder to address issues when they inevitably arise. But accountability doesn't have to feel confrontational. When you use a coaching approach, these interactions become more respectful, constructive, and solution-focused. Even if you typically avoid conflict, leaning into these conversations with a coaching approach—focused on curiosity, clarity, and ownership—can help you shift from an amateur mindset to a more professional, proactive leadership style; one that feels respectful while simultaneously focusing on results.

MASTERING THE ART OF PURPOSEFUL MEETINGS

Poor planning, unclear goals, ineffective facilitation, and lack of follow-up are some of the biggest reasons meetings often feel like a waste of time. Most of us have sat through meetings where valuable ideas were shared, yet nothing came of them. You leave thinking progress was made, but without action or follow-through, that time is ultimately lost. To make meetings truly effective, you need a clear purpose, and everyone in the room should understand what you're there to accomplish.

In many organizations, poorly run meetings lead to even more meetings, just to resolve issues that weren't addressed the first time. The goal should be to maximize the return on time spent. When you consider the combined hourly pay of everyone attending, the cost of an unproductive meeting adds up quickly. That's why intentional, well-structured meetings are essential for clarity, alignment, and results.

FRAMEWORK FOR SUCCESSFUL MEETINGS

To facilitate a productive meeting, focus on three essentials: **Clarity, Purpose,** and **Accountability.**

Meetings become significantly more effective when there's clarity around the goal and the right people are in the room. One of the most common mistakes professionals make is scheduling a meeting without a defined objective, resulting in scattered conversation and little to no meaningful action.

As David Allen, author of *Getting Things Done*, emphasizes, every meeting should start with a clear purpose.[52] Meetings exist for a reason—whether it's to make a decision, generate ideas, share information, or solve a problem. If the purpose isn't clear, the meeting probably isn't necessary.

Finally, accountability is non-negotiable. A meeting that ends with vague intentions but no ownership or follow-through is a missed opportunity. Productive meetings should always result in clear action items, assigned responsibilities, and agreed-upon next steps.

5 MINUTES TO CLARITY METHOD

I've developed a method that I teach to my clients to maximize their meeting time and deliver significant results.

In as little as five minutes, you can set up a meeting that is purposeful and successful.

If you are the organizer of the meeting, the questions below will help you prepare for a successful meeting.

Preparing for a Meeting: Questions to Clarify Purpose and Focus

- What is the specific purpose of this meeting? What outcome do we need to achieve?
- Is a meeting the best way to accomplish this goal, or could it be handled more efficiently through another format (e.g., email, shared document, quick check-in)?
- Who truly needs to be in the room to contribute or decide—and who can be informed afterward?
- What key decisions need to be made during this meeting?

Once you have determined the purpose, create an agenda and communicate the specifics of the meeting to participants, including any information they need to research, prepare, or present. Part of the time wasted in meetings is when people don't know what is expected. You can leverage the time by being clear about any pre-work.

At the Start of the Meeting

- State the goal or outcome of the meeting and write it somewhere visible, like a whiteboard, screen, or printed agenda.
- Identify the key decisions that need to be made.

This simple step sets the tone, creates clarity, and helps everyone stay aligned. When the conversation starts to drift, you can confidently guide it back to the intended focus. It's also helpful to have a whiteboard or easel nearby to capture unrelated ideas or questions—a "parking lot" for items that can be revisited later without derailing the meeting.

I recommend having someone in the meeting take high-level notes. The notetaker should feel empowered to stop at any point to clarify the following:

- What action are we committing to?
- Who is responsible?
- When is the due date?

While generating ideas and exploring solutions is valuable, none of it matters if there's no follow-through. Without clear action steps, even the best discussions become wasted time.

END OF MEETING RECAP

An essential part of any effective meeting is the end-of-meeting recap. Reserve the last five to ten minutes of the meeting to turn discussion into action. Use this time to review key takeaways, confirm responsibilities, and ensure clarity on what happens next. This step is critical for facilitating follow-through and maintaining accountability.

Consider the following questions to guide your recap:

- What are the key decisions or takeaways from this meeting?
- Who is responsible for each action item?
- What are the deadlines or timelines?
- What needs to be communicated—and to whom?
- By when should that communication take place?

Capturing and confirming these details ensures alignment, prevents miscommunication, and keeps momentum moving forward.

The best results will come from this method when the entire organization is adopting it. When you receive a meeting request without an agenda, reply to the organizer and politely ask for one so you can properly prepare for the meeting. If you are an executive in your company, I encourage you to implement these best practices and permit employees to decline meetings without an agenda. This may sound bold, especially if an employee is invited to a meeting by a leader with a higher-level position, but it's an effective way to reinforce the value of each person's time. When employees feel empowered to take charge of their time, you will experience powerful results by reducing wasted time and frustration, while improving communication, productivity, and engagement.

Facilitating results as a leader is about creating the conditions where accountability, ownership, and follow-through become the norm. It is not about micromanaging or enforcing compliance through fear, but about setting clear expectations, building strong structures, and modeling the behaviors you want to see in your team.

Accountability starts with you: how you communicate, how you follow through on commitments, and how you handle challenges when expectations are not met. By fostering a culture where accountability is seen as a path to growth rather than a tool for blame, you empower employees to take responsibility for their work and contribute at a higher level. When leaders commit to clarity, consistency, and constructive coaching, they elevate both individual and team performance, creating impactful and lasting results.

CONCLUSION:
THE ELEVATED LEADER

The wisest mind has something yet to learn.

—George Santayana

After talking with a friend at school, my son Luca came home last year excited to play hockey. A longtime Washington Capitals fan, he had always been interested in the sport, but became really interested in playing after learning his friend was on a team. I was open to the idea, so I started looking into how we could enroll him.

What I found was a lot more involved than I had anticipated. There were several prerequisites before he could even step onto the ice for a game. He had to start with a Pre-Hockey Skills 1 class, which would take six weeks. After passing a skating test, he could move on to Pre-Hockey Skills 2 for another six weeks, followed by another test, and then finally, the tryouts for the team.

As I began explaining the process to Luca, I noticed his excitement start to fade. As I walked through the details, the frustration on his face grew. When I finished, he yelled, "I just want to play hockey! I don't want to do all of that. I don't want to take a class or a skating test. I just want to play hockey!"

This moment with Luca reminded me of a quote from my favorite baseball player, Derek Jeter of the New York Yankees: "You don't accidentally show up in the World Series." Achieving something great doesn't happen by chance—it takes consistent effort, daily discipline, sacrifice, and dedication.

As leaders, we must recognize that this is true for us, too. The work of leadership is never finished.

Exceptional outcomes don't happen by accident; they're built through effort, discipline, and intention. Just like you don't show up and make the hockey team without preparation and hard work, you don't create an exceptional team or company culture by chance. In leadership, it's not holding the title or stepping in occasionally that matters most—it's the consistent, everyday actions. And while it can feel overwhelming at times, it's the leaders who stay actively engaged—who follow through, communicate with intention, and show up consistently—who earn trust, build a great culture, and achieve results.

As I reflect on my own leadership journey—from mastering the technical intricacies of HR to stepping into a leadership role, I've realized one profound truth: learning never stops. Leadership isn't a destination; it's a dynamic, ever-evolving process. Each day presents opportunities to grow, adapt, and refine your approach—not just for the benefit of your team, but for your own personal and professional fulfillment.

Leadership and society are constantly evolving. The workplace of today is not the same as it was five, ten, or twenty years ago—and it won't be the same five years from now. New technologies, shifting expectations, and evolving societal and cultural norms continue to redefine what it means to lead effectively. As a leader, it's your responsibility to remain curious, embrace change, and approach every challenge with a mindset of growth and adaptability.

The strategies I've shared in this book are not only meant to elevate your leadership, but your life as well. The goal isn't just to produce more at work or to check off tasks from a never-ending to-do list. It's about approaching your leadership and work with intention and impact so you can create the kind of life you truly love. Leadership isn't just about producing results; it's about creating a balance that allows you to thrive both at work and in your personal life.

Leadership is an influence that extends far beyond the individual. When you elevate how you lead, you not only increase your impact on your team, but you also enhance the quality of your own life. By cultivating self-awareness, building authentic connections, and leading with clarity and intention, you create a ripple effect that allows others to grow and succeed. And as your team thrives, so do you—experiencing greater fulfillment, purpose, and alignment in your work and life. Because the true

> LEADERSHIP IS AN INFLUENCE THAT EXTENDS FAR BEYOND THE INDIVIDUAL.

reward of leadership isn't just in the results, it's in the growth it sparks in everyone, including yourself.

But let's be clear: this isn't easy work. It takes energy, effort, and intention to move beyond the comfort zone of technical expertise and step into the broader responsibilities of leading people. It requires you to confront your own limiting beliefs and habits, embrace self-awareness, and continually strive for better. But the impact is powerful: engaged teams, meaningful relationships, and a sense of purpose that extends far beyond the workplace.

As you close this book and take your next steps, remember that leadership is about progress, not perfection. Every day is a chance to do better, learn more, and lead in a way that inspires and empowers those around you.

As we look ahead, it's time to rethink how we identify and promote leaders. Leadership isn't just a promotion or a reward for high performance; it's a distinct profession that demands a unique skill set, a growth-focused mindset, and a deep responsibility to develop others and facilitate results.

Too often, organizations promote people based on tenure or technical expertise, overlooking a candidate's capacity to inspire, coach, and guide people. The consequence is a cycle of mediocre—or even toxic—leadership that erodes performance, culture, and morale.

To break this cycle, we must be more discerning and thoughtful about who we put in leadership positions. This requires setting higher standards for leadership and ensuring that those who step into these roles are not just capable but truly prepared—both in skills and mindset—to lead others with integrity, clarity, and purpose.

It's time to raise the standards we have for leadership.

We have the opportunity, and the responsibility, to redefine what leadership looks like by being intentional in how we choose, equip, and support leaders. When we raise the standard, we create stronger teams, healthier cultures, and better results.

So here's the challenge: Commit to elevating your leadership, not just for your team, but for yourself. When you lead with clarity, integrity, and confidence, you don't just create a positive impact at work—you create a life of greater intention and influence.

***You* have the power to elevate your leadership, your team, and your life.**

FINAL THOUGHTS

While I wrote this book to provide managers with strategies for building confidence, influence, and impact as leaders, my deeper intention is to help you channel your focus and energy in a way that supports living fully, not just leading effectively. This isn't about squeezing more tasks into the day. It's about making intentional choices with your energy and focus so you can build a thriving career alongside a fulfilling, joyful life.

For that to be possible, organizations must do their part as well. By preparing and training managers before they are promoted, and by advancing only those with the skills to truly lead, we set leaders up for success rather than overwhelm. When organizations invest in their managers, they don't just build stronger leaders; they create workplace cultures that are sustainable, healthy, and that support wellbeing both at work and at home.

A theme running through these pages is the shift from amateur to professional. Amateurs wait for perfect conditions to do the hard work, chase urgency, and let the day dictate their priorities. Professionals, on the other hand, set clear priorities, design their days with intention, and commit to small disciplines that compound over time. They protect their focus, delegate effectively, and coach their teams rather than carry everything themselves. They accept that some days will bring unexpected challenges, but they anchor themselves in principles that form the foundation of effective leadership. An Elevated Leader recognizes that when you lead like a professional, intention becomes leverage—fewer distractions, more high-value work, clearer boundaries, and steadier progress, even in the busiest seasons of life.

We only have so much capacity, and leadership shouldn't require every ounce of it for work. Many managers are also working parents who want to be present in their children's lives, not watching those moments slip away because of long hours and overwork. As a mom of three, I know firsthand that there are sacrifices and tradeoffs to working full-time. And while I'm not suggesting leaders can always limit their workweek to 40 hours, the inspiration for this book is built on the belief that with intention, it is possible to leverage your time and succeed at both.

As a working parent, some days I feel like a rockstar, and some days I feel like I'm hanging by a thread. Like everyone, I have days when I feel overwhelmed and stressed. And in those moments, I return to the principles that ground me. Asking myself, "What is the most important thing I should be working on right now?" has become a touchstone question in my life.

No day will ever be perfect; there will always be demands, tradeoffs, and sacrifices. But when leaders approach their work with clarity and purpose, they can create space for meaningful leadership *and* a fulfilling personal life. The tools in this book are designed to help you set clear priorities, protect your focus, and build margin, so you can elevate your leadership and your life.

In the middle of writing this book, my nine-year-old son, Luca, became ill. What started as a few weeks of fatigue and unexplained symptoms quickly turned into countless doctor visits, blood work, and sleepless nights filled with worry and uncertainty. After what felt like an endless stretch of questions without answers, we finally learned in August 2022 that Luca had Crohn's disease, a chronic condition that would require ongoing care and management.

The year following his diagnosis was one of the most challenging of my life. My son was my priority, but I didn't have the luxury of stepping away from my business, and I had responsibilities as a parent of three. Balancing it all—while navigating doctor visits, the insurance company, and medication changes—was often exhausting.

I quickly learned that I needed to focus intensely at work to create the margin to navigate everything else.

As anyone who has faced a health crisis, a family challenge, or a difficult season can attest, your priorities become unmistakably clear. That season reinforced why I believe so strongly in leading with intention: because when we protect our energy and focus, we not only lead more effectively, but we also preserve the capacity for what is most important in our lives. Luca's health challenge is also where my mantra, "Be With What Is," came to be. I realized that staying stuck in those emotions wasn't helping me or him. Over time, I learned to move through them and refocus on what I could control. From that place of presence and clarity, I was able to best support Luca.

Just as I had to reset and refocus during that season, leaders must do the same. Exceptional leaders pause to reflect regularly, creating space to recalibrate and realign with what matters most. One practice I find impactful is a simple exercise I return to twice a year.

- What do I want **more** of in my life?
- What do I want **less** of?
- What is my **preferred future**?

My answers to these questions guide the next six months. Over the last five years, my "more of" list has often included more peace, downtime, and margin in my schedule. While that is not always easy to implement in a busy life, refocusing myself on the areas that create more joy and fulfillment helps me to strive for a more balanced life. I want to enjoy life along the way, whether it's savoring my morning cappuccino, playing cards with my daughter Clara, reading a great book, or enjoying our family vacation. Those are the most meaningful moments in life.

It's normal to go through seasons where you struggle, doubt yourself, or feel weighed down by challenges. Every leader and every person experiences times when confidence wavers or direction feels uncertain. Your inner critic can flood your mind with fear and negativity, but your inner coach can guide you back to clarity and confidence. In those moments, I've found it grounding to turn to a simple practice: I ask my future self, my 80-year-old wiser self with a broader perspective, what to do next. Connecting with my older, wiser self helps me see past the immediate pressures and make choices that serve the bigger picture of my life.

As you close this book, my hope for you is that you not only elevate your leadership, feel confident leading your team, and gain practical strategies to succeed, but also acquire tools and perspective to elevate your personal life. May you create a life of joy and impact—one where your work is meaningful, your relationships are strong, and your choices reflect the future you most want.

True success is not only being an elevated leader, but also living a life you love.

ENDNOTES

1   John Harrison, "Managers Play a Key Role in Employee Mental Health: Here's How You Can Support Them," WebMD Health Services, April 18, 2023, https://www.webmdhealthservices.com/blog/managers-play-a-key-role-in-employee-mental-health-heres-how-you-can-support-them/.

2   Tonya Eckert, "Managers Impact Our Mental Health More than Doctors, Therapists - and Same as Spouses," Global Press Release & Newswire Distribution Services, January 24, 2023, https://www.businesswire.com/news/home/20230124005390/en/Managers-Impact-Our-Mental-Health-More-Than-Doctors-Therapists-and-Same-as-Spouses.

3   Jim Harter, "U.S. Employee Engagement Sinks to 10-Year Low," Gallup.com, January 14, 2025, https://www.gallup.com/workplace/654911/employee-engagement-sinks-year-low.aspx#:~:text=In%20the%20latest%20reading%2C%20from,than%202020's%20high%20of%2036%25.

4   Trista, "40 Basic Rights Women Did Not Have until the 1970s," History Collection, June 26, 2019, https://historycollection.com/40-basic-rights-women-did-not-have-until-the-1970s/.

5   Emily Field et al., "Stop Wasting Your Most Precious Resource: Middle Managers," McKinsey & Company, March 10, 2023, https://www.mckinsey.com/capabilities/people-and-organizational-performance/our-insights/stop-wasting-your-most-precious-resource-middle-managers.

6   Steven Pressfield, *Do the Work* (La Vergne, TN: Sanage Publishing House, 2023).

7   Dwight D. Eisenhower, "Remarks at the National Defense Executive Reserve Conference, 11/14/57," Quotes | Eisenhower Presidential Library, accessed April 28, 2025, https://www.eisenhowerlibrary.gov/eisenhowers/quotes#:~:text=%22I%20tell%20this%20story%20to,%2C%20but%20planning%20is%20everything.%22.

8   Stephanie Franks, "Distress vs Eustress," American Psychological Association, 2023, https://www.apa.org/ed/precollege/topss/lessons/activities/critical-thinking-exercise-distress-eustress.pdf.

9   Kimberly Holland, "Amygdala Hijack: What It Is, Why It Happens & How to Make It Stop," Healthline, April 18, 2025, https://www.healthline.com/health/stress/amygdala-hijack.

10   "Well-Being, N. Meanings, Etymology and More," Oxford English Dictionary, accessed April 28, 2025, https://www.oed.com/dictionary/well-being_n?tl=true.

11   "Covid-19 Pandemic Triggers 25% Increase in Prevalence of Anxiety and Depression Worldwide," World Health Organization, March 2, 2022, https://www.who.int/news/item/02-03-2022-covid-19-pandemic-triggers-25-increase-in-prevalence-of-anxiety-and-depression-worldwide.

12   Dr John Delony, Building a Non-Anxious Life (Franklin, TN: Ramsey Press, 2023).

13   Cyril Northcote Parkinson, "Parkinson's Law," The Economist, November 19, 1955, https://www.economist.com/news/1955/11/19/parkinsons-law.

14   "Study Breaks & Stress-Busters," Cornell Health, accessed August 18, 2025, https://health.cornell.edu/about/news/study-breaks-stress-busters; Kirsten Weir, "Give Me a Break," Monitor on psychology, January 2019, https://www.apa.org/monitor/2019/01/break#:~:text=Breaks%20can%20improve%20our%20moods,deal%20with%20the%20daily%20grind.%E2%80%9D.

15   Amy Gallo, "What Is Psychological Safety?," Harvard Business Review, February 15, 2023, https://hbr.org/2023/02/what-is-psychological-safety?utm_medium=paidsearch&utm_source=google&utm_campaign=domcontent_leadership&utm_term=Non-Brand&tpcc=domcontent_leadership&gad_source=1&gclid=Cj0KCQiAwvKtBhDrARIsAJj-kTg7uUjVEYuwKH_og2d4N6_2moFGeKHGQnG7iGw7dAVOJQVByTq8-MQaAtm1EALw_wcB.

16 "How the CLIFTONSTRENGTHS Assessment Works," Gallup.com, December 17, 2024, https://www.gallup.com/cliftonstrengths/en/253676/how-cliftonstrengths-works.aspx.

17 "Achiever," Gallup.com, December 17, 2024, https://www.gallup.com/cliftonstrengths/en/252134/achiever-theme.aspx.

18 Elena Doldor, Madeleine Wyatt, and Jo Silvester, "Research: Men Get More Actionable Feedback than Women," Harvard Business Review, February 10, 2021, https://hbr.org/2021/02/research-men-get-more-actionable-feedback-than-women.

19 Michael Hyatt and Megan Hyatt Miller, *Win at Work and Succeed at Life: 5 Principles to Free Yourself from the Cult of Overwork* (Grand Rapids, MI: Baker Books, 2021).

20 Pavithra Mohan, "These CEOS Work 40 Hours or Less a Week (and Think You Should Too)," Fast Company, August 30, 2019, https://www.fastcompany.com/90385364/these-ceos-work-40-hours-or-less-a-week-and-think-you-should-too.

21 Ibid.

22 Adele Peters, "Why Sweden Is Shifting to a 6-Hour Workday," Fast Company, September 29, 2015, https://www.fastcompany.com/3051448/why-sweden-is-shifting-to-a-6-hour-work-day.

23 Arianna Stassinopoulos Huffington, The Sleep Revolution: Transforming Your Life, One Night at a Time (New York, NY: Harmony Books, 2017).

24 Christopher M. Barnes, "Sleep Well, Lead Better," Harvard Business Review, September 1, 2018, https://hbr.org/2018/09/sleep-well-lead-better.

25 Jeff Hyman et al., "Take 5: How to Keep Your High Performers Happy," Kellogg Insight, May 2, 2018, https://insight.kellogg.northwestern.edu/article/take-5-how-to-keep-your-high-performers-happy#:~:text=While%20most%20people%20know%20superstars,time%20as%20their%20neighbors%20changed.

26 Linda Stone, "Beyond Simple Multi-Tasking: Continuous Partial Attention," Linda Stone, November 30, 2009, https://lindastone.net/2009/11/30/beyond-simple-multi-tasking-continuous-partial-attention/.

27   Tori DeAngelis, "Too Many Choices?," Monitor on psychology, June 2004, https://www.apa.org/monitor/jun04/toomany.

28   Fast Company Staff, "Leading Ideas: Know What NOT to Do," Fast Company, September 30, 2005, https://www.fastcompany.com/672403/leading-ideas-know-what-not-do.

29   Brian Tracy, *Eat That Frog!: 21 Great Ways to Stop Procrastinating and Get More Done in Less Time* (Oakland, CA: Berrett-Koehler Publishers, Incorporated, 2017).

30   Gary Keller, *The One Thing* (London, UK: Hachette Book Group, 2013).

31   "Multitasking: Switching Costs," American Psychological Association, March 20, 2006, https://www.apa.org/topics/research/multitasking.

32   Susan Weinschenk, "The True Cost of Multi-Tasking," Psychology Today, September 18, 2012, https://www.psychologytoday.com/us/blog/brain-wise/201209/the-true-cost-of-multi-tasking.

33   Realization, "Study: Organizational Multitasking Costs Global Businesses $450 Billion Each Year," PR Newswire: press release distribution, targeting, monitoring and marketing, August 26, 2013, https://www.prnewswire.com/news-releases/study-organizational-multitasking-costs-global-businesses-450-billion-each-year-221154011.html.

34   John Pencavel, "The Productivity of Working Hours," Stanford University & IZA, April 2014, https://docs.iza.org/dp8129.pdf.

35   Brian Tracy.

36   Steve Glaveski, "10 Quick Tips for Avoiding Distractions at Work," Harvard Business Review, December 18, 2019, https://hbr.org/2019/12/10-quick-tips-for-avoiding-distractions-at-work.

37   Susie Cranston and Scott Keller, "Increasing the 'meaning Quotient' of Work," McKinsey & Company, January 1, 2013, https://www.mckinsey.com/capabilities/people-and-organizational-performance/our-insights/increasing-the-meaning-quotient-of-work.

38   Karen Tiber Leland, "You Could Be Your Own Biggest Interruption. Here's How to Stop and Find Your Focus | Inc.Com," Inc., August 12, 2019, https://www.inc.com/karen-tiber-leland/you-could-be-your-own-biggest-interruption-heres-how-to-stop-find-your-focus.html.

39   "The Impact of Interruptions," UC Berkeley, accessed April 29, 2025, https://hr.berkeley.edu/grow/grow-your-community/wisdom-caf%C3%A9-wednesday/impact-interruptions.

40   "Forgetting Curve," ScienceDirect Topics, accessed April 29, 2025, https://www.sciencedirect.com/topics/agricultural-and-biological-sciences/forgetting-curve.

41   Brené Brown, "Clear Is Kind. Unclear Is Unkind.," Brené Brown, October 15, 2018, https://brenebrown.com/articles/2018/10/15/clear-is-kind-unclear-is-unkind/.

42   Dan Sullivan and Benjamin Hardy, *Who Not How: The Formula to Achieve Bigger Goals through Accelerating Teamwork* (Carlsbad, CA: Hay House, Inc, 2020).

43   Shannon Waller, "Overcoming Delegation Issues: A 5-Step Guide," Strategic Coach, accessed June 2, 2025, https://www.strategiccoach.com/resources/the-multiplier-mindset-blog/overcoming-delegation-issues-a-comprehensive-5-step-guide.

44   "State of the Global Workplace Report," Gallup.com, April 25, 2025, https://www.gallup.com/workplace/349484/state-of-the-global-workplace.aspx.

45   Denise McLain and Ryan Pendell, "Why Trust in Leaders Is Faltering and How to Gain It Back," Gallup.com, April 17, 2023, https://www.gallup.com/workplace/473738/why-trust-leaders-faltering-gain-back.aspx.

46   Elisa Boxer, "Home Depot's CEO Did This 25,000 Times. Science Says You Should Do It Too," Inc., November 10, 2017, https://www.inc.com/elisa-boxer/home-depots-ceo-did-this-25000-times-science-says-you-should-do-it-too.html.

47   Gary D. Chapman and Paul E. White, *The 5 Languages of Appreciation in the Workplace: Empowering Organizations by Encouraging People* (Chicago, IL: Northfield Publishing, 2019).

48   Susan Scott, *Fierce Conversations: Achieving Success at Work & In Life, One Conversation at a Time* (New York, NY: Berkley, 2004).

49   Roger Connors, Tom Smith, and Craig R. Hickman, *The Oz Principle: Getting Results through Individual and Organizational Accountability* (New York, NY: Portfolio, 2010).

50   Henry J. Evans, *Winning with Accountability: The Secret Language of High-Performing Organizations* (Dallas, TX: CornerStone Leadership Institute, 2008).

51   Loom, Inc. "New Data: Workers Spend Almost Half Their Day Communicating, Making It Difficult to Actually Get Work Done," GlobeNewswire News Room, April 27, 2023, https://www.globenewswire.com/news-release/2023/04/2 7/2656566/0/en/New-Data-Workers-Spend-Almost-Hal f-Their-Day-Communicating-Making-It-Difficult-To-Actually-Get-Work-Done.html.

52   David Allen, *Getting Things Done: The Art of Stress-Free Productivity* (New York, NY: Penguin Books, 2014).

ACKNOWLEDGMENTS

Writing this book has been one of the most rewarding and challenging journeys of my life, and it would not have been possible without the support, encouragement, and inspiration of many people.

Thank you to the managers throughout my career who have had an impact on me, including Chris Rampe, Vinny Rampe, Ray Henry, Robert Falcone, Dave Joy, Dawn Palmer, Linda Ramsey, Thom Beck, and especially Debra Fry, who provided me with many opportunities and whose support and encouragement were invaluable.

With deep gratitude to the thought leaders whose work has profoundly influenced both my personal growth and professional path: Tony Robbins, Darren Hardy, Marie Forleo, Kevin Cashman, Patrick Lencioni, Mel Robbins, Ryan Holiday, Dr. Brené Brown, Steven Pressfield, and Dan Sullivan.

Thank you to Jack Canfield, who has been a wonderful mentor and a huge inspiration not only professionally but also personally. The principles I learned from you continue to have an incredible impact on my life.

To my amazing clients: I am grateful for your trust, your partnership, and the opportunity to work with you as you make an impact in your organizations.

Thank you to Sheila Trask, whose guidance and thoughtful questions helped me to shape my ideas for this book.

To my editor, Jill Ellis, who offered thoughtful suggestions and helped bring clarity and strength to the ideas, structure, and voice throughout this book. To the publishing team, especially Kary,

Melissa, and Jamie, thank you for your guidance and support in bringing my ideas to the world.

Robbie Samuels–thank you for your support in helping me launch this book in a strategic and impactful way.

To the staff at Hillbrook—especially Carissa, Becky, Lisa, Cathy, Jessi, Julie, and Mark. Thank you for your warm hospitality. Hillbrook became my creative haven, and it's where the majority of this book came to life. The space allowed me to disconnect from the noise and fully immerse myself in the writing process, and for that, I'm deeply grateful.

To my amazing team, especially Lisa Stafford, who has been a wonderful support for me and my business. Jalene and Emma—thank you for your creativity, support, and commitment to excellence.

To Rino—from the beginning, you have been my biggest supporter. Thank you for believing in me, encouraging me, and making it possible to step away and pour myself into this book. I know that sacrifices were made so I could pursue my dreams, and I am deeply grateful to have such a supportive and loving husband and best friend.

To my three wonderful children–Olivia, Luca, and Clara. You are my purpose, my joy, and my greatest inspiration, and I am so proud to be your mom. I love you all so much.

Finally, to every reader who picks up this book: I hope these ideas spark something meaningful for you and that you implement them in ways that elevate your leadership and your life.

ABOUT THE AUTHOR

Laurie Maddalena is a professional keynote speaker, certified
executive coach, and leadership
development consultant on a
mission to transform workplace
cultures and rid the world of bad
management practices. As the
founder and CEO of a leadership development consulting firm,
she provides leadership development programs for managers and
executives, executive coaching,
management training, and leadership assessments.

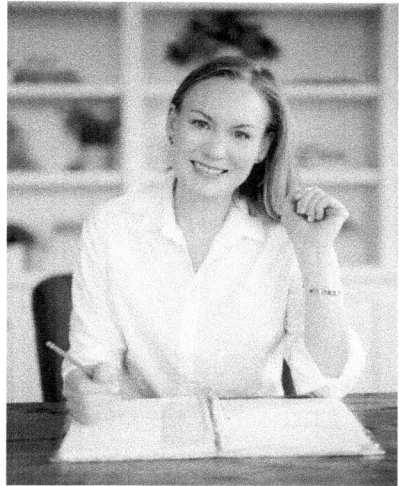

Laurie is a member of the National Speakers Association (NSA)
and is a Certified Speaking Professional (CSP), a distinction earned
by less than 17 percent of speakers worldwide. She is a contributing
author to the international best-selling books, *Women Who Empower*
and *Women Who Shine*.

Laurie has worked directly with Jack Canfield and is a certified
Success Principles Trainer. She has also worked with Brené Brown,
a bestselling author and researcher.

Prior to establishing her own coaching and consulting business,
Laurie served as Vice President of Human Resources/Organizational
Development at Montgomery County Teachers Federal Credit Union.
Under Laurie's leadership, the credit union was awarded the "Excellent

Place to Work" designation by the Maryland Work-Life Alliance for seven years in a row.

Laurie earned a Master of Business Administration (MBA) and a Master of Science degree in Human Resources and Organizational Development from the University of Maryland Global Campus. She earned a bachelor's degree in speech communication and rhetorical studies from Syracuse University. Laurie is a certified executive coach through The Coaches Training Institute and completed team and organizational coaching training through The Center for Right Relationship and Team Coaching International.

Laurie lives in Maryland with her husband, Rino, and their three children, Olivia, Luca, and Clara. She loves nature, cappuccinos, and a nice glass of Cabernet Sauvignon, and is an avid reader.

Elevate Your Leadership By Mastering Coaching

MAKE THE SHIFT FROM MANAGING TASKS TO LEADING PEOPLE.

DOWNLOAD LAURIE'S FREE COACHING GUIDE

LaurieMaddalena.com/Free-Guides

LEADERSHIP INSIGHTS FROM LAURIE

Receive Tools and Strategies to Elevate Your Leadership and Your Life

LaurieMaddalena.com

THE ELEVATED LEADER PROGRAM

PERSONAL WELLBEING

Self Awareness

Reflection

INTERNAL ELEMENTS

Energy

Intention

EXTERNAL ELEMENTS

Create Clarity

Facilitate Results

Caretake the Culture

ORGANIZATIONAL WELLBEING

LEARN THE SKILLS TO LEAD CONFIDENTLY, COACH EFFECTIVELY, AND CREATE A THRIVING TEAM.

LaurieMaddalena.com/ElevatedLeader

www.ingramcontent.com/pod-product-compliance
Lightning Source LLC
Chambersburg PA
CBHW071556210326
41597CB00019B/3276